# The Cheshire Baby Whisperer™

# Ultimate sleep guide for babies & toddlers

by Evelyn Burdon, RN, RM, RHV, BSc

The Cheshire baby whisperer ultimate
sleep guide for babies and toddlers
is written and published by Evelyn Burdon
copyright ©2014 Evelyn Burdon

First edition 2014
Second edition 2015

I am very proud to dedicate this book
to two special women in my life:
my beautiful daughters, Sophie and Emma.
They are my greatest achievement.

# Contents

# Acknowledgements

I've been passionate about sleep, not only as a health professional but also as a parent, as I too experienced sleepless nights, sleep deprivation and craved sleep.

The book was first published in 2014 and the feedback and response from parents has been very rewarding. Within months of publishing I was itching to add more information and I am delighted to include a new section on day naps and co-sleeping breastfed babies for the second addition.

I want to thank Clare, my loyal and inspirational best friend, for sharing my dream and passion, and Sophie and Emma, my daughters, for their encouragement and enthusiasm.

# Foreword

Our baby was four months old and I felt a bit embarrassed that we'd got things so wrong that we had to call in an expert. After all, parenting is meant to come naturally and it wasn't our daughter's fault that she'd been taught all the bad habits in her short life. But as with anything else, if you don't have the expertise to do something yourself, you hire a professional, so why would sleep be any different? Sleep is a basic human need, not an optional luxury, and to be persistently deprived of it is unhealthy at best and dangerous at worst.

When I started Evelyn's Multi-Sensory Techniques, I would say that I was sceptical, but desperate, to start with! I had read *The Baby Whisperer* (Tracey Hogg), Gina Ford and quite a lot online, especially on Mumsnet. I am quite an organized, systematic person who likes to be in control so I decided this was how I would approach things. It did not really occur to me that my baby might not see the world in this way!

I also believed that the only way to get rid of the dummy and teach self-settling would be to undergo controlled crying. We thought we had the hideous choice of surviving broken nights until she was six months old, or doing it when she was still very young. I was so relieved that following the Multi-Sensory Sleep Techniques was a gentle solution, much quicker and more effective than I thought possible, without the heartache of leaving our baby crying and distressed.

I definitely had no idea how much babies need to be taught in order to sleep or how obsessed with sleep I would become. I have always liked my sleep and knew it would be hard. Luckily, Jack copes a lot better than me! I don't think I was very naïve, but it was massively more difficult than I thought and definitely contributed to feeling quite negative and, at times in the early weeks, pretty unhappy. I am sure lack of sleep contributes to postnatal depression. While I haven't suffered from it myself, I think many mums do experience some form of it. I can say with certainty that I started to enjoy Isla a lot more when she started to sleep better. I also think that, easy as it is to get into bad habits, with your Multi-Sensory Techniques, it is also easy to get out of them. Babies are quite adaptable.

I was a bit worried, at first, that playing in the nursery would give the wrong message. Now, I think it makes total sense. We really tried to make the nursery a nice and fun place to be. Previously we removed her from fun downstairs when she was tired and grumpy and took her to her nursery. This made sleep seem like a punishment! Now, we have sensory play time in the nursery with favourite toys and I sing her favourite songs. The techniques are actually simple and I suppose I thought, "*Yeah, we've tried that,*" (for instance, putting a muslin that smells of you in the bed). But we had not done the total sensory approach. I had taken her to a baby sensory room before, which she had enjoyed, and relaxed in. I just hadn't really thought of using the same approach ahead of sleep.

I had wondered if the lights and music would become another sleep prop, but it does not seem to be the case. Sometimes, I will see her on the video monitor stir and wriggle and then go back to sleep, which is satisfying as I know she is resettling herself. I think the fear of SIDS makes you worry about putting your baby in her own room and putting anything in the cot. Although we had put her in her own room, I had all her cuddly toys sitting on a shelf, not snuggled in her bed with her. She definitely likes to manhandle them as part of going to sleep. I usually see her waving her monkey around in her hands! The Slumber Buddy was also a surprise hit. We'd used Ewan the Dream Sheep before, but he hadn't made much impact, whereas she's definitely drawn to the glow of the frog (we wave it around as we get her dressed, which seems to keep her calm).

Probably, the other thing I would say is that sleep and getting my evenings back with my husband are a big part of feeling normal again. It's so nice to have dinner together and even a glass of wine (only on a Friday night!).

**Suzie Henriques**

Here is what Jack had to say:

I was at work on Monday when my wife called me around 1pm.

*"OH, MY GOD!"* she said. *"She's AMAZING!"* (Note to Evelyn – I'm not just saying that for dramatic effect – those were her actual words.) On her first visit, Evelyn had done what we hadn't managed in weeks to get Isla to go to sleep without a dummy. We were over the moon and realising that it was possible for Isla to do that, was a huge milestone. We followed Evelyn's advice, and as she promised, over the next couple of nights, we heard less and less from our beloved little demon. Not only did she learn to get herself back to sleep without the dummy, but she seemed to be waking less in the first place.

A few weeks later, the dummy is long forgotten. We've had some other sleep-related issues with Isla, but Evelyn has always responded to emails and phone calls straight away to guide us. Her help has been invaluable. This gave us the confidence we needed to continue taming of the beast. My wife and I both feel we are more in tune with Isla and better able to recognise her needs thanks to the support we've received from Evelyn.

**Jack Henriques**

# Introduction

Are you sleep deprived and exhausted?

Is your baby waking three to four times a night?

Are you at the end of your tether?

Do you want to take control of your baby's sleep problem?

**Help is at hand!**

Being a new parent is exhausting and many parents experience a sleep problem in the first two years of their baby's life. Most parents appreciate help with a baby/toddler sleep problem and my approach to sleep is not only baby-led but also parent empowering.

Hello, my name is Evelyn Burdon welcome to my Multi-Sensory Sleep Techniques and Sleep Routines. My interest in baby/toddler sleep started thirty years ago when, in the mid-1970s and early 1980s, I trained as a nurse, midwife and health visitor. Every week, mums came into my baby clinic asking the same question: *"How can I get my baby to sleep?"* Mums listened intently while I gave them sleep advice, but what they really wanted was practical help at bedtime. When I retired in 2011, I became an independent practitioner, the Cheshire Baby Whisperer™. Within a week of advertising, I was driving to my first baby-whispering visit and since then I have visited hundreds of parents. Being a physical presence in the nursery meant that I could support parents and help them choose positive sleep associations for their baby. This was a unique and privileged experience.

It led me to devise my Multi-Sensory Approach to sleep based on:

- Child development
- Scientific sleep research
- Sensory sleep associations
- Common sense

More importantly, they work, and within days the sleep problem is resolved.

With each success, I wanted more parents to benefit from my techniques. In June 2013, I was fortunate to meet a young filmmaker, David Parry, and together we made a sleep training DVD for babies and toddlers entitled *Sweet Baby Dreams*. The DVD has been very successful. Here are just a few of the wonderful comments I have received:

*"I would like to thank Evelyn Burdon aka the Cheshire Baby Whisperer for helping with Archie's routine. It has deffo worked and I would recommend it to any parents who are struggling with a sleep routine."* **Debbie Bamford.**

*"After going almost insane with a lack of sleep for a whole year, I do believe we have a sleeper, an actual 7pm – 7am sleeper. Yep, SLEEP, real SLEEP. I could weep with joy. I feel like a normal human being. Evelyn, you are a total genius!"* **Anne Scott.**

*"Evelyn Burdon is amazing. To all mums that need advice or help with their child's sleep, she is a genius. Thank you Evelyn."* **Felicity Hallett.**

*"Evelyn I can not thank you enough, your help and support has been amazing, your DVD is so easy to follow and makes perfect sense. You have saved my family and this morning our baby woke happy and content just like his parents."* **Catherine Lever.**

*"Thank you so much Cheshire Baby Whisperer, that's the first day time nap where Harvey has self-settled & in his own cot as well!! This routine is a winner."* **Katie Turner.**

*"I can't thank you enough for all your support and advice – I have gone from being convinced I had a little boy who just wouldn't sleep to having a little boy who goes down so quickly and sleeps through the night – the difference in such a short time is incredible. Thank you just doesn't cover it."* **Lindsay Greathead.**

I continued to receive e-mails from sleep-deprived parents and this was the motivation I needed to write about my experiences. There are many parenting books and books about controlled crying, strict routines and rules that dominate and take over your life. My book is different. It is about:

- Sleep from your baby's perspective
- What your baby is feeling and thinking as he drifts off to sleep
- How to make positive sensory sleep associations for your baby/toddler
- How to maintain peaceful sleep

**What is a sleep association?**

From the moment babies are born, they learn about their parents and their environment through the senses of smell, sound, sight, touch and taste. Babies make sleep association soon after birth. Whatever your baby sees, feels, smells, tastes, and hears while they drift off to sleep will become either a positive sleep association or a negative sleep association. All five senses are in the same area of the brain as memory and emotion. This is why some perfumes or some music can evoke a powerful emotional memory from our past. My Multi-Sensory Sleep Techniques and Routines use the same principle to create a sleeping environment that stimulates the senses to produce a memory of peace and tranquility prior to sleep. By implementing my techniques, you will understand sleep from your baby's perspective and appreciate how your baby:

- Interacts with you
- Communicates with you
- Adapts to the sensory world around them
- Makes sleep associations
- Reaches their maximum sleep potential

My Multi-Sensory Sleep Techniques and Routines transform lives. I am confident this book will give you the knowledge and skills to resolve your own complex and difficult baby/toddler sleep problem. I hope you enjoy reading it as much as I enjoyed writing it. Key to my approach is gentle perseverance, patience and persistence. In addition, you will learn how to:

- Create the perfect sleeping environment for your baby/toddler
- Implement simple and effective sleep routines for your baby/toddler
- Prevent sleep problems occurring
- Solve an existing sleep problem
- Recognise your baby's personality and how personality influences sleep
- Manage bedtime with a new sibling
- Understand how weaning affects sleep
- Identify and resolve specific sleep problems related to breastfeeding

To every parent who trusted me and invited me into their home, **thank you.**

Good luck and I wish you many peaceful nights.

If you were to read this book cover to cover you will notice I have adapted the sensory techniques and routines to take into account the different developmental stages of babies. In each chapter there are subtle but significant changes, which will inevitably lead to repetition. I recommend you read: Why is Sleep Important, Baby-led Sleep, Parenting Styles, Multi-Sensory Sleep Techniques and then the chapter for the relevant age of your baby. If you cannot find the answer to your problem it will be in Chapter 16, Frequently asked questions, on page 253.

# Chapter one

# Why is sleep important to human health?

*"The consequences of baby sleep problems can have long lasting detrimental effects on all family members."*

Quality sleep is vital for human health. Humans have biological rhythms, known as circadian rhythms, which control our body clock. Poor quality sleep can cause a circadian rhythm sleep disorder, which is linked to ill health and prolonged periods of sleep deprivation can have a detrimental effect on all the family. Lack of sleep causes accidents, tiredness at work, loss of concentration, irritability and frayed tempers.

During the last three months of pregnancy, women experience disturbed sleep, which increases the risk of antenatal and postnatal depression and puts extra stress on parental relationships. After the birth, tired and depressed mums are less able to interact with their baby in a positive way, which interferes with mother/baby bonding. In addition, there is a link between postnatal depression and behavioural problems in children. If you are interested in reading more about postnatal depression, I recommend Elaine Hanzac's *Eyes Without Sparkle*, in which she documents her experience of postnatal depression and her downward spiral into puerperal psychosis. We have spoken several times and Elaine is convinced that her depression was exacerbated by her baby's unresolved sleep problem.

The consequences of baby sleep problems can have long lasting detrimental effects on all family members. In fact, parents rate their child's sleep problem more stressful than dealing with a health problem. Tired and stressed parents are often too exhausted to untangle the complicated behavioural problems associated with sleep. Therefore, it is essential that parents have a clear knowledge and understanding of sleep, as they are part of the problem and the solution.

The rest of this chapter contains information from infant sleep research studies conducted in America and Australia.

### In this chapter:

- Sleep cycles, REM and Non-REM
- Sleep patterns in pregnancy
- Sleep patterns in the unborn baby and after birth
- How long can my baby sleep for?
- Sleep disturbance: nightmares and night terrors

### Sleep cycles

All babies and adults experience two distinct sleep patterns: REM, or Rapid Eye Movement, and Non-REM.

### REM

Babies experience two cycles of REM during night sleep, one at the start of sleep and one at the end. During REM:

- Adults and babies are in light dreaming sleep
- The brain reprocesses daily events necessary for our mental wellbeing
- The baby grows and develops
- Infant brain development occurs, which is important for intelligence

## Non-REM

Most adults and babies are in Non-REM sleep between midnight and 4am. Non-REM sleep is much deeper and more energising than REM sleep.

### During Non-REM:

- The human body repairs and regenerates itself
- There is an increase in the production of hormones
- There are increased levels of the milk hormone prolactin, vital for breastfeeding mums

### Sleep patterns in pregnancy

Pregnant women often suffer from circadian rhythm sleep disorder in late pregnancy. Following research into the sleep patterns of pregnant women and their unborn babies, Koukis (2009) and McNamara (2012), reported that pregnant women:

- Experience more REM sleep than Non-REM
- Can detect the movements of their baby whilst in REM
- Are easily woken by anxiety dreams
- Have dreams about losing control, aggressive animals, deep waters, waves, animal births and various images of the child

### Sleep patterns in the unborn baby and after the birth

Unborn babies sleep 90% of their time in REM. Babies' sleep and breathing patterns are synchronised with their mother but soon after birth, mother and baby sleep patterns diverge and their breathing patterns are no longer synchronised.

### REM and Non-REM sleep cycles

Every baby is born with their own unique sleep potential, which is the total number of hours they can sleep in a day, with the average being 12 hours in a 24 hour period. The ratio of REM to Non-REM changes during the first year.

Taking 12 hours as the average, I calculate that babies' ratios of REM to Non-REM sleep are as follows:

| Age | In REM | In Non-REM | Ratio |
| --- | --- | --- | --- |
| **Newborns** | 10.2 hours | 1.8 hours | 85:15 |
| **Three-months** | 9.6 hours | 2.4 hours | 80:20 |
| **Six-months** | 8.4 hours | 3.6 hours | 70:30 |
| **Nine-months** | 7.2 hours | 4.8 hours | 60:40 |
| **One-year** | 6 hours | 6 hours | 50:50 |

Generally, babies have one period of Non-REM sleep, from midnight until 4am. All babies either rouse or wake up at the transition from REM to Non-REM sleep and vice versa. In my experience, without exception, if babies are rocked, cradled or fed to sleep they wake up in REM, rouse to consciousness, cry out and need to be resettled. However, babies who can self-settle at the start of sleep without being rocked, cradled or fed to sleep can re-settle themselves without parental intervention. Your baby's day naps are in REM sleep.

### How long can my baby sleep for?

Every healthy baby has the ability to sustain a period of unbroken sleep. The age related sleep potential without waking (for healthy babies) is as follows:

| | |
| --- | --- |
| **One month** | 3-4 hours |
| **Three months** | 8-9 hours |
| **One year** | 10-11 hours |

My Multi-Sensory Sleep Techniques and Sleep Routines enable babies to attain their age related sleep potential.

# Sleep disturbance

Nightmares and night terrors tend to occur in older babies and toddlers when children are unwell or have a high fever. In my experience, some children are predisposed to having nightmares and night terrors: they are naturally very imaginative, physically active toddlers, 'always on the go' and have difficulty relaxing at bedtime.

## Nightmares

A nightmare is a bad dream and occurs in REM sleep. Babies cry in REM sleep and if a bad dream wakens your little ones, they are distressed, frightened and cling on to you. The best response is to comfort, cuddle and reassure them. Switch on the night light and sit and wait in their room until your baby/toddler is relaxed and sleepy enough to go back to sleep. Avoid taking your baby/toddler out of their bedroom to sleep with you as this is counterproductive and will confuse your child. If you are aware that your child has difficulty relaxing at bedtime, implement my Multi-Sensory Sleep Techniques and Sleep Routines.

## Night terrors

In my professional experience, night terrors are vivid dreams occurring in REM sleep. Children who have night terrors are still dreaming, but appear to be awake; sometimes the child acts out the dream and will point to an object only they can see. The child's actions and appearance differ from those relating to a nightmare: they are unresponsive, staring ahead and not making eye contact; sometimes babies will cry and toddlers will babble and say the odd word. Picking up and cuddling does not reassure your child and the advice from specialists is not to waken them. Stay with your child, hand them their comforter/teddy and wait until the dream passes.

You can read more information about nightmares and night terrors in Chapter nine: What to expect in babies one- to two-years-old, on page 147.

## Conclusion

When you appreciate how vital sleep is to your health, the health of your baby and the general well-being of all the family, you will want to ensure that you implement good sleeping patterns from the very beginning. I recommend parents synchronise their baby's sleeping pattern to one that suits their lifestyle. However, this will only happen if your baby/toddler has made positive sleep associations. These are the cornerstones and central to my Multi-Sensory Sleep Techniques and Sleep Routines.

Some sleep problems can be caused by medical conditions, such as colic or reflux and I cover health problems that affect sleep in chapter 14. However, most sleep issues can be attributed to parenting behaviour, i.e. how the parent interacts and responds to their baby at the onset of sleep and during the night.

Now is the time to implement my Multi-Sensory Sleep Techniques and Sleep Routines to create positive sleep associations for your child.

# Chapter two

# Baby-led sleep

*"Some babies get into the habit of only sleeping when held
or fed, this being the main cause of a sleep problem."*

Quality sleep for all the family ultimately leads to contented babies and relaxed and happy parents. Therefore, one important aspect of caring for your baby is where and how your baby settles to sleep as it has a significant influence on your baby's sleep potential. Baby-led sleep involves releasing your baby's unique sleep potential and allowing your baby to lead their sleep; your baby will signal to you when they are ready to go to sleep. Every baby is capable of a unique number of sleeping hours within any 24 hours.

## In this chapter:

- Tired or just bored?
- Adapting to change
- Causes of sleep problems
- Understanding your baby's cry
- Tired baby cry
- Positive change

### Tired or just bored?

I am aware that some parenting books recommend that babies should be encouraged and made to have a day nap every two hours. If babies resist and 'fight' their sleep, this results in parents using various coercive techniques, such as feeding to sleep, rocking to sleep, 'shush/pat' and 'pick up put down'. Coercing babies to go to sleep does not take into account babies' differing personalities and stages of development. Following a sleep trainer's strict rules undermines the parents' confidence and ability to recognise when their baby is tired or just bored. My Multi-Sensory Sleep Techniques and Sleep Routines are baby-led, not parent-led.

Parents are encouraged to learn:

- How to understand what their baby is saying to them
- How to identify a bored baby as opposed to a tired baby
- How to respond to their baby's tired cry

### Adapting to change

Before you begin making any changes to your baby's sleep routine, take note that I do not agree with, or advocate, leaving a baby to cry. Listening to a crying baby is stressful for adults, even those without children and it is completely unnatural and inappropriate in every case. In addition, parents worry that leaving their baby to cry is harmful and neglectful; the idea of leaving your own baby to cry will seem intolerable. I believe that my Multi-Sensory Sleep Techniques and Sleep Routines are a viable alternative to controlled crying. The methods are also baby friendly and parent empowering.

### Causes of sleep problems

Babies do not understand what is happening when changes occur in their environment and their natural response is to cry and to communicate how they feel. How parents react and respond to their baby's cry has a significant influence on whether their baby continues to cry or stops crying. Most babies stop crying when they are picked up, rocked, shushed or fed; parents then feel pleased and satisfied when they have soothed their baby to sleep.

Some babies get into the habit of only sleeping when held or fed, this being the main cause of a sleep problem, which can continue for months and even years. Tired parents are desperate for sleep and will do anything to settle their baby as quickly as possible. Parents who contact me are confused why their baby settles so easily with a feed or a cuddle at bedtime but wake frequently through the night. The parents quickly realise they are part of their babies settling process and once they teach their baby how to self settle without a feed or cuddle at bedtime their babies sleep through the night.

### Understanding your baby's cry

All babies cry. Crying is the baby's form of communication and they express emotions using a variety of cries. Some babies are more vocal and expressive than other babies, my oldest daughter daughter cried much more than her sister and, 26 years later, she is still a chatterbox and a great communicator!

My Multi-Sensory Sleep Routines are baby led and this empowers parents to recognise that babies use various cries to get their parents attention. It is the first stage of language development and encouraging parents to interpret, empathise and understand what their baby is saying to them.

### Tired baby cry

Until your child can express in words what they want, their cry is the first form of communication, with each cry having a different meaning. In my experience, it is quite difficult to identify what babies under three months old want as they have an identical cry for food, attention, discomfort and sleep. For the first three months, it is a process of elimination; try a cuddle first, then offer a feed until the baby is relaxed and content. Fortunately, after three months the difference between a hungry baby and a tired baby is easily recognisable.

The Multi-Sensory Sleep Techniques and Sleep Routines help parents to recognise the natural 'tired baby' cry – this is the cry that all babies make when they are tired. The tired baby cry is quiet in volume, whiny and 'mantra' sounding. Often there is an element of frustration in the cry, associated with lots of yawns and eye rubs. It is not a distressed cry; your baby's eyes are closed and there are no tears. The cry can vary in strength, length and volume, depending on your baby's personality. Some tired babies can sound quite angry and frustrated, but do not be afraid of your baby's cry. Learn what they mean so that you can respond appropriately: when your baby makes this cry, he is close to sleep. My Sleep Techniques work best when your baby is making the tired baby cry as this cry signals the start of the sleep routine.

### Positive change

All babies are born with the capacity for their natural sleep potential and, within days, have accepted and adjusted to the new routine. Parents who contacted me for help had been suffering sleep deprivation for months, were completely exhausted and did not know where to turn to for help. Parents should not feel they have failed if they ask for help – in fact, the opposite is true, so be positive. All the problems I encountered were either: the babies had made a sleep attachment to milk, breast or bottle, or had become dependent on the feel, touch and smell of their mum at every sleep time. In all situations, mum was the main sleep attachment. Although it is very important to make strong attachments to their mum, babies can sleep independently.

Parents are part of the problem and part of the solution; my advice is to stand back and allow your baby to learn how to self-settle. Through observation, I discovered that success or failure in the process depends entirely on the parent's behaviour and attitude towards the new routine. There can be differences and disagreements with couples over what is tolerable and what needs to be changed. I have met dads who feel pushed out of the marital bed by their baby son. In contrast, I have met mums who prefer sleeping alone with their baby. The sleep problem may not concern the partner/spouse if they are getting a full eight hours' rest, sleeping in the spare room. However, most couples are not happy sleeping separately and want help before it becomes a permanent arrangement and affects parental relationships.

I suggest that you now read about my Multi-Sensory Sleep Techniques and Sleep Routines. They will:

- Help your baby to make positive sleep attachment
- Teach your baby to self-settle
- Allow your baby to reach his maximum sleep potential

# Chapter three

# Multi-sensory sleep techniques

*"Babies start to use their senses before birth: your unborn baby has been listening to your voice for months."*

This chapter is about sleep from your baby's perspective. I advocate a baby-led approach to sleep that is baby-friendly and parent-empowering.

> **In this chapter:**
>
> - How your baby interacts with his sensory world
> - How babies make sleep attachments
> - How to make the nursery multi-sensory
> - How to help your baby make positive sleep attachments and associations to sound, sight, smell, touch and taste

From birth, your baby is communicating with you and learning about their environment using all the five senses. Your baby's memory and emotions are stimulated by the senses and this is how babies learn to make either positive or negative associations to everything in their life. I use the term 'multi-sensory' as babies learn to make sense of their immediate environment using multiple senses.

## How your baby interacts with his sensory world

Your tiny newborn baby looks so helpless, it is hard to imagine that their personality and ability to learn is already in place and waiting to emerge. Within a few weeks of birth, your baby is interacting and communicating with you and this is a wonderful bonding experience for you both. Babies start to use their senses before birth: your unborn baby has been listening to your voice for months and, after the birth and your baby will stop crying when he hears your voice. Babies are born with a heightened sense of smell and hearing and will make sucking and licking movements with their tongue and lips when they smell their mother's breast milk.

Familiar sounds, sights, smell, touch, and taste are comforting and reassuring for babies. Positive sleep attachments ensure your baby maintains peaceful sleep throughout the night, while negative sleep attachments will prevent your baby reaching their maximum age-related sleep potential.

## How babies make sleep attachments

Babies use all their senses when they drift off to sleep and each sense will have a sleep association. For example, if your baby falls asleep at the breast at every sleep time, this encourages your baby to have a sleep attachment to the breast and nipple (you). Consequently, your baby will need you to be available at every sleep time and during the night. Imagine what your baby sees, feels, smells, tastes and hears when falling asleep in your arms: your smell and scent, the sight of your smiling face, the sound of your soothing voice, your gentle touch, the oral sensation of the nipple in baby's mouth and the taste of your breast milk.

All five senses will become deeply ingrained sleep associations for your baby. Although it is very important to establish strong mother-baby bonding in the first weeks of your baby's life, babies are capable of making positive sleep associations to a comforter/teddy, a soft glow light, or soothing womb sounds instead.

By observing your baby while awake and asleep, and stimulating and playing with your baby, you are engaging your baby's senses and encouraging their development. Learning about your baby's sensory attachments and associations will increase your understanding and confidence about what your baby wants and feels. Thus, the parental bond is strengthened.

# How to make the nursery multi-sensory

Most parents plan the nursery months ahead of the delivery. It is a lovely time, and when the baby has arrived, most nurseries are set up and ready to go. Even though babies sleep in the same room as mum and dad for several months, the nursery is used every day, initially for changing and, occasionally, feeding. Your baby will only make a positive attachment to the nursery if it is used every day. I recommend parents spend sensory play time in the nursery with their baby from birth. As you will be in the room too, make it sensory and colourful with sparkly lights. I recommend parents spend sensory play time in the nursery with their baby from birth.

**To make the nursery multi-sensory, I suggest the following:**

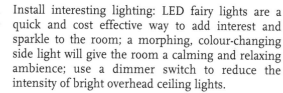

- Install interesting lighting: LED fairy lights are a quick and cost effective way to add interest and sparkle to the room; a morphing, colour-changing side light will give the room a calming and relaxing ambience; use a dimmer switch to reduce the intensity of bright overhead ceiling lights.

- Make room for a comfortable, padded chair that supports your back whilst feeding and is big enough to sit in with your baby when he/she is older.

- Choose a cot appropriate for your needs: some cot-beds are too big and bulky to fit into the parents' room, which means that babies sleep in a Moses basket for much longer than is recommended by the manufacturers – 12lbs is the limiting weight for some baskets. If you are planning to room-share with your baby, I recommend that you look at a range of smaller cots for one that will initially fit into your bedroom and can be transferred to the nursery later.

Make the nursery sensory with sparkly lights

Fit battery operated cot mobile such as the Rainforest Mobile

Attach a battery operated mobile to the cot and switch it on while you are in the room; very young babies do not like objects directly over their faces, so sit your baby on your knee and look at the mobile together, until he becomes accustomed to it.

 Play music while you are in the room.

The rest of this chapter will look at how to make positive sleep associations for your baby using the five senses.

# Smell

Babies have a very acute sense of smell and, within days of the birth, can easily recognise their mother's scent. A familiar smell can soothe and comfort a baby; it is therefore a good idea to scent all new clothing, bedding and blankets with your familiar scent as it will calm and comfort your baby. There are aromatherapy oils that aid sleep; if you prefer to use these, add one drop of oil to a sleep teddy/blanket/comforter.

### How to give a comforter positive sleep-smells

Babies will often make sleep associations with comforters and little blankets designed for babies to use in their cot whilst asleep. Babies do not choose to make an association with a sleep teddy/comforter; they will only make a positive attachment if the comforter is used during a feed and sleep time. I recommend that breastfeeding mums put a comforter within their bra whilst breastfeeding as this will give baby the opportunity to smell and touch the comforter while he feeds. The comforter can then be attached to the cot whilst your baby sleeps and the smell of the comforter will quickly become a positive sleep-smell association. It will settle and relax your over-tired, restless baby and be a constant reminder of you. Comforters are ideal for very sensitive babies who cry more than other babies and take longer to settle in new environments.

## Choice of comforter

Decide which sort of comforter you would like your baby to have as the attachment to a comforter lasts a long time. The comforter will be whatever your baby feels during a feed and when drifting off to sleep: it could be your breastfeeding muslin, bra-strap, clothing label, scarf, T-shirt, or nightie. Babies will choose their own comforter and it might not be what you expect; I remember one toddler had made a sleep attachment to his mum's pink silky nightdress and carried it everywhere, even to baby clinic.

## Advantages

A comforter can reduce the stress of taking your newborn baby to new places and will also help the transition from your bedroom to the nursery. To encourage a positive sleep-smell association with the nursery and cot, keep the comforter in the cot during the day and only use it at sleep times; with this method, I have noticed that older babies and toddlers are less trouble and actually look forward to going to bed and being reunited with their teddy/comforter. In addition, if you keep the teddy/comforter in the cot, you know where it is and there is no danger of losing it. Never underestimate how attached babies can be to a teddy/comforter; I know many parents who still have their first teddy.

This is a direct quote from a mum who implemented my Multi-Sensory Sleep Techniques and Sleep Routines:

> "We left our bunny at nursery yesterday. Night time was absolute hell! Instead of our perfect baby snuggling down after his bath... suddenly we had a monster! As soon as he got out of the bath he started asking for it, so I gave him a 'back up', but he looked at me as if I'd given him road kill! It took over two hours for him to finally go off (at 9.45pm). Then he was awake at 12.30am, 1.30am, 2.30am, 4am (for an hour) 5.30 (for an hour) and then slept until 7.50am, so we were late for nursery! What a night! I have never been so relieved to be reunited with a piece of fluffy material in my life... thinking of getting it insured! Thanks again for all your help. It just shows what a difference these little things make!" **Sophie Dickens.**

48

Young children like repetition and often choose the same bedtime story

Use LED fairy lights to add interest and sparkle to the room

## Negative smells to avoid

Not all smells are positive sleep associations. Be aware of negative sleep-smell associations, as babies are more sensitive to room smells than adults; every room in your house will have a different odour and they can affect your baby's sleep. Some smells, such as cooking odours, are too stimulating for babies, as they will wake and rouse a sleeping baby, stimulating their instinct to root for milk; this is noticeable in very young babies who wake up and cry every time they smell food. To prevent your baby waking at your mealtime, move your sleeping baby to your bedroom before you start cooking; your baby will sleep for longer and you will be able to enjoy your meal in peace.

Avoid letting your baby sleep in the lounge during the day as it has a complicated mix of strong odours. If babies sleep in the lounge every day, those babies will develop a sleep-smell association to that room and babies who regularly sleep in the lounge are then restless and wakeful in the bedroom at night. To reduce this problem, let your baby sleep in your bedroom for a day nap as this will reinforce the sleep association with your bedroom, which will have a very familiar comforting smell. If you are concerned about leaving your baby to sleep on his own, set up the baby monitor with a camera to give you peace of mind.

### Summary: How to make positive sleep-smell associations

- Introduce a comforter from birth and impregnate it with your personal scent
- Only use a comforter at sleep times to reinforce a positive sleep-smell association
- Leave the comforter in the cot or bed to encourage your baby into the cot or bed at sleep times
- Ensure your baby has a day nap in the room in which they sleep at night

Sound

### Positive sleep-sounds for newborn babies

The first sounds that babies hear are womb sounds: your voice, heartbeat, whooshing and gurgling sounds, muffled voices and music. A favourite position of newborn babies is lying face down on your chest where they can hear and feel the heartbeat. Babies stop crying when parents whisper in their ear, and rouse from REM sleep when they hear their mother's voice.

### Sleep-sounds

Music has an important role in sleep associations and if you play calming sounds, such as sounds from nature, or classical music, at sleep times, the sound will become a positive sleep association. Sea and ocean sounds are very relaxing and hypnotic; after hearing the sound/music four to five times, your baby will develop a sleep attachment and every time they hear the sound/music, they will become relaxed and calm. Turn the sound/music off once your baby is asleep, otherwise the sound will permeate into your baby's unconscious mind and they will become too reliant on the sound during sleep. Also available are sleep toys that mimic womb sounds and heartbeat which can be used in sleep association.

### Nursery rhymes

Play nursery rhymes in the nursery while you are changing baby, carrying out baby massage or reading stories as this creates a positive attachment in the nursery and will help calm and relax babies who suffer from colic and reflux. Vary the music to distract your over-tired and fractious baby. Play nursery rhymes during sensory play before the bath but then switch to your relaxing, hypnotic sleep-sounds after bath time to signal that this is the start of the bedtime routine.

### Transfer from bedroom to nursery

When your baby moves from your bedroom to the nursery, do not

A morphing colour changing light will give the room a calm ambience

Slumber Buddy Butterfly with a red glow light and hypnotic sea sounds

forget to take the music with you. A mum recently told me that her baby loved the musical mobile, but when she removed the mobile section from the cot she also removed the music unit, not realising that her baby had made a sleep-sound attachment to it. When she reattached the music unit to the cot, her baby recognised it and settled off to sleep straight away. This highlights the fact that parents are not always aware of the influence that sleep-sound associations have on their babies' sleep.

### Child rearing practices

Britain's child rearing practices have changed over the decades and now very few babies have a day sleep in their pram outdoors. However, it is still common practice in Scandinavia to let babies sleep outside, even in winter. I visited a family from Finland, and their baby was having all her day sleeps outside, but found at bedtime they could not settle her and she cried. They were very relieved when they found a sleep toy that played garden bird sounds, and were amazed when she immediately relaxed and settled to sleep!

Babies like listening to sounds, but as they get older, toddlers tend to prefer listening to stories whilst lying down in bed. Stories at bedtime are a wonderful and relaxing end to their very busy day; young children like repetition and often choose the same bedtime story and they especially love to hear stories about themselves when they were little. Lovely chats at bedtime will become their favourite part of the bedtime routine.

### Sounds to avoid

New babies are very sensitive and will startle and cry at loud noises; too much noise overstimulates and confuses babies, causing them to become fractious and restless. Therefore, I recommend that you do not leave your baby sleeping near the television or computers as sleep studies have shown that electronic equipment can affect the quality of sleep.

### Noisy environments

Some babies become accustomed to sleeping in noisy environments, but are then unable to sleep at night because it is too quiet. This is very common in premature babies who have been in a neonatal unit and in babies born into families with noisy toddlers and older children. I have known some parents who have left the television or radio switched on during the night just for the baby. If your baby sleeps better with some background noise, play nature sounds and gradually lower the volume until your baby can settle without sound.

Older babies, although not startled by loud noises, are very inquisitive and easily distracted by television and sleeping in front of the television can seriously disturb their sleep patterns and maximum sleep potential. Any distracting noises will prevent your baby entering a deeper, more rested sleep and they wake up sooner. Catnaps are great for cats, but not for babies, and your baby will wake up still tired and very grumpy!

### Summary: How to make positive sleep-sound associations

- Introduce a soothing sleep sound from birth and play it at every sleep time
- Turn off the sleep sound as soon as your baby is asleep
- Read to your baby at every sleep time

## Sight

Newborn babies are sensitive to intense bright light, and sight is the least mature of the newborn's senses; they look cross-eyed when focusing on an object. Your baby can see blurry images, shapes and outlines and will focus on your face from a distance of six to eight inches. They like black and white patterns, bright primary colours and will stare intently, mesmerised by ceiling lights.

### How to make positive sight-sleep associations

The sleep hormone, melatonin, is produced in darkness; therefore, darken the bedroom at naptime and your baby will sleep for longer. In the summer months, a blackout blind will certainly help to darken the bedroom. Your very young baby will be sleeping in your bedroom for the first months, but still use interesting lights as it will help make a positive sleep-sight association; you can later transfer the lights to the nursery. Choose a morphing, colour-changing night light or a light that projects moons and stars on the walls and ceiling; a soft red glow light is very calming for young babies.

### Visual stimulation for babies three months old

By three months of age, your baby's vision is perfect and your baby will watch everything that goes on nearby; this is the time to brighten up the nursery with battery operated LED fairy lights that will help make the nursery interesting and create positive sleep-sight associations. Your baby will enjoy spending time in the nursery, they will cry less and they will be much easier to settle in the cot. Some night lights project stars on the walls and ceiling, making the nursery 'womb-like with stars'. Many parents believe that lights will overstimulate their baby, but, in my experience, this is not the case. The lights entertain babies until they are rubbing their eyes and yawning, which is the sleep cue to turn off the fairy lights and leave a soft red glow light on. I have seen hundreds of babies gaze dreamily at a deep red glow light, it attracts their attention, then, after a while, they close their eyes and drift off to sleep. Switch off all lights once your baby is asleep.

### Cot mobiles

A cot mobile is a great introduction to a positive sleep-sight association as it develops eye coordination and entertains a restless young baby. Avoid wind-up mobiles, as they are often very bland and look boring; instead, choose a mobile that comes in two parts: a base unit that fixes to the cot and plays a variety of sleep sounds, and a mobile part that can be detached when your baby is able to sit up and reach it. Young babies will lie in their cot, gazing up at the mobile, peaceful and relaxed, distracted from crying, mesmerised by the movement and pattern of the mobile. Your baby may not go to sleep watching the mobile, but will have entered a very relaxed sleepy state and gained some experience of self-settling. Babies who learn how to self-settle and self-soothe become independent sleepers and achieve their maximum sleep potential. Until your baby likes lying down and looking up at moving objects, sit your baby on your knee and look at the mobile together. Do not leave the mobile on if the baby is very upset; that would produce a negative association towards the mobile.

### Toddlers

I have observed that as babies get older, they lose interest in projectors and light shows, but they still like interesting lights. Older babies love the Slumber Buddies, and they are ideal for toddlers too. Pictures and paintings on the walls, books on shelves and toys in boxes make a cosy, calming bedroom atmosphere at bedtime. Avoid leaving stimulating toys in your toddler's bedroom; they will attract your baby's attention and entice him out of bed to play. The room should be as calming and as tidy as possible, so move toys out of sight into boxes or cupboards.

**Summary: How to make a positive sleep-sight association**

- Darken the bedroom with blackout blinds to produce the sleep hormone melatonin
- Introduce a soft red glow night light from birth
- Brighten the nursery with lights that project stars on the walls and ceiling
- Tone down or switch off the brighter lights and just use a soft red glow light when your baby is ready to sleep
- Switch off all lights as soon as your baby is asleep

## Touch

### Positive loving touch

'Skin to skin' contact is a vital bonding experience for a mother and her new baby. Many babies appear to relax when swaddled in a single layer blanket, designed for swaddling, it gives babies a 'womb-like' feeling of security. Most, but not all, babies like being held and cuddled and some mums have commented that their baby did not like to be held; some babies are simply not cuddly babies. Most newborns appear to like having their head, face, hands and feet touched so I recommend learning about baby massage. Classes, with trained experts, can be found in most towns and villages. If you want to have constant close physical contact with your baby, you can use a sling from birth, but wait six weeks if you have had a C-section.

### Positive touch and safe sleeping area

The recommended sleeping position for newborn babies is on their back in a Moses basket, crib or cot. However, there is a newborn reflex called the Moro reflex, which causes babies to startle, flail their arms out, wake up and cry. To prevent the Moro reflex disturbing your baby, gently hold your baby's arms while they lie in the cot until relaxed. If you are having trouble settling your baby in the Moses basket, try the following technique: while your baby is relaxed, but not asleep, position your baby in the cot or Moses basket, slightly to one side; place a very soft cot-teddy behind your baby and attach the scented comforter to the cot or basket, near enough so that the baby can feel the softness on their face. If your baby is restless and wriggly, gently hold your hands either side of your baby's body and stroke your baby's face. Do this until your baby is relaxed and drifting off to sleep; it is very important that you stay in the room with your baby. When your baby is asleep, remove the teddy, attach the comforter safely to the Moses basket and leave your baby on his back. If you repeat this at every sleep time, your baby will learn how to self-settle and sleep to his unique sleep potential.

### Negative sleeping areas

There are some sleeping places to avoid, such as the car seat, bouncy chair or play mat. Prolonged day naps in them will prevent your baby reaching their maximum sleep potential at night.

By eight weeks old, most babies are too big for Moses baskets, most of which are only suitable for babies who weigh less than 12 lbs.

As soon as your baby can touch the sides of the Moses basket, that is the cue to move your baby to a cot, as touching the sides often wakes babies who were previously sleeping through the night. Moving your baby to a cot is a positive move, as the child will have more freedom and space to wriggle about. In addition, fresher, more oxygenated air circulates in a cot.

From four months, your baby's sleeping position will change. Babies are now physically very active and start to roll over onto their tummy. Once they have achieved it, many babies prefer to sleep in that position. This is quite normal infant development, and if your baby has good head control and can raise his head and shoulders off the mattress, it is perfectly safe for your baby to sleep on his tummy.

### Positive touch and comforter

I recommend that you introduce a comforter from birth and place it where your baby can feel it at every feed and sleep time; if you persist with a comforter, within a few weeks your baby will have made a positive attachment to it. Most six-month-old babies are very tactile and enjoy feeling and scratching different fabrics and textures: they rub their face and eyes when they are tired and will grab hold of your clothing while they are feeding. If you have not introduced a teddy/comforter at sleep time, now is a good time to do so, as your baby will rub their face with it at sleep time and it will become a positive sleep association. Otherwise, your baby will choose a negative sleep-touch association, such as stroking your hair, holding your hand, or wanting to be patted or rocked to sleep. Older babies are so much easier to settle at bedtime and sleep for longer when they have a comforter.

### Positive touch at bath time

A bedtime bath is a positive sleep-touch association. During the bath, the skin cools and after the bath, the body starts to heat up, causing a warm, cosy effect; relaxing hormones are released, which make babies calm and sleepy after a bath. Babies and toddlers should go straight into bed before the warm, cosy effect of the bath is lost. Not only does the ritual of the bath signal bedtime, it also uses up the last amount of energy.

Although bathing your baby is positive sleep-touch association, your newborn does not find the bath a particularly relaxing experience, as babies do not like the insecure feeling of their skin exposed. Newborn babies lose heat very quickly; therefore, to make the experience more pleasurable, warm the bathroom first. If you have a dimmer switch in the bathroom, dim the lights and fill the baby bath with warm water at 36-38°C; special baby bath thermometers are useful for this. Babies like the water to cover their abdomen, and specially shaped baby bathtubs are designed for this. If your baby's skin is very dry, plain water can aggravate the condition; therefore, use a dermatologist-recommended moisturising baby wash such as Diprobath, Epaderm, Hydromol bath, or Oilatum: pharmacies sell them without a prescription. During my home visits, I observed that babies who went swimming were confident in the bath and did not mind water splashing on their faces. If you are planning to take your baby swimming, check out baby swimming classes.

### Summary: How to make positive sleep-touch association

- Settle your new baby to sleep in the Moses basket when drowsy, but before they are asleep
- Give your baby something to touch at sleep time, such as a soft comforter or teddy
- Use the cot from eight weeks old
- Make bath time part of the bedtime routine

# Taste

**Negative sleep taste association**

Within minutes of birth, babies are encouraged to feed at the breast or take a bottle of formula. A milk-sleep association is normal in healthy, full term newborn babies and babies up to one month old and they spend the first few weeks in a milky, sleepy haze. However, after a month or two, babies' feeding time is reduced quite dramatically, as they can feed more efficiently.

There are two types of sucking actions: nutritive and non-nutritive. In my experience, babies like to do both, and after a feed they enjoy a few minutes of non-nutritive sucking. However, as babies get older they often develop a habit of falling asleep at the breast or bottle, using the sucking action to soothe them to sleep. This is a negative sleep association, is not an easy habit to break and prevents babies reaching their unique sleep potential.

In Australia, a breastfeeding study revealed that 66% of six-month-old babies were likely to wake during the night and that 72% were unable to sleep alone. The conclusion was that the babies were falling asleep at the breast, and had developed a negative sleep-milk association. In my experience, discouraging a milk-sleep association does not compromise breastfeeding in any way. It is quite normal and healthy for exclusively breastfed babies to self-soothe and then sleep for six hours during the night without waking for a feed.

### Positive sleep taste association

The easiest way to stop a negative milk-sleep association is to change the time when the feed is given. Avoid sleepy feeds, as your baby is not alert enough to feed properly. Aim to feed after a day nap, not before, and this will encourage efficient feeding; your baby will be more awake and alert and will feed efficiently, thereby increasing the amount of milk intake. Consequently, the feed will be more satisfying. Babies over three months old can have their last milk feed in the lounge before the bath.

When your baby is having three meals a day, substitute the last milk feed for either yogurt, which is just as nutritious as milk, or rice cereal and mashed banana. Your aim is to reduce the risk of a milk-sleep association, but there is another valid reason behind this advice: breast milk and formula milk contain sugar and will cause tooth decay if given to babies after they have brushed their teeth. Your dentist will advise you that once your baby has reached 12 months, drinking sugary liquid, including milk, from a bottle, increases the risk of dental caries as the enamel in babies' teeth is soft.

**Dummies**

Babies who have a dummy have an oral dependency on it. Parents have commented to me that a dummy settles their baby very easily, but within an hour the dummy has fallen out and their baby has woken up, crying. This is very frustrating and tiring for the mum, and results in broken sleep for the baby too. To reduce the dependency on the dummy, only give it to your baby at sleep time, and remove it once your baby is asleep. The medical profession has made a link between prolonged dummy usage and ear infections, which is another reason to 'ditch the dummy'.

**Summary: How to prevent a negative sleep-taste association**

- From two to three months old, settle your baby for a day nap without a feed
- Offer milk feeds when your baby wakes up from a day nap
- Avoid feeding when your baby is tired
- Avoid comfort breastfeeds
- Only use a dummy at sleep time
- From two to three months, give the last feed, breast/bottle, before the bath

I recommend you read Parenting Styles next.

# Chapter four

# Parenting styles and personality traits

*"Parenting should be child-centred; if baby is happy, then mum, dad and the rest of the family will be happy too."*

I worked as a health visitor in a small town in Cheshire for many years. Health visitors are part of the community primary health care service that all families receive when they have a new baby. Being in this unique and privileged position, I met families from all sections of society and observed, at first hand, the dynamics of family life. This gave me knowledge, insight and understanding about most parenting issues. I quickly realised that not every parent is a 'natural' and they experience a mixture of emotions as babies do not come with a 'How to' manual! How you were parented, and what you observed in other families, will influence your parenting style, and every parent aspires to be a 'good parent'.

During the pregnancy, most new parents never imagine they will have a sleep problem. They are protected from such thoughts by looking at the future through 'rose tinted glasses'. When they do experience a baby sleep problem, some parents worry that they have failed their baby and have done something wrong; guilt, embarrassment and fear can stop parents seeking help. Realising that there is a problem should never be thought of as being a bad parent or as a failure in any way. The opposite is true. Parents who ask for help are very conscientious and caring mums and dads. Changing patterns of behaviour, accepting that there is a problem and taking responsibility, is a challenging and brave act. Untangling a complicated sleep problem is not easy, but a little guidance is always helpful. The parents I met wanted help, and appreciated practical step-by-step information and solutions to resolve their baby's sleep problem. It is my mission to give you the knowledge and confidence to resolve your baby/toddler sleep problem.

**In this chapter:**

- Dad's involvement
- Attachment Parenting
- Babywise Parenting
- How your baby's personality can affect sleeping patterns

There are hundreds of parenting books to choose from and parents often search for a particular parenting style to suit their personality. My parenting style is based on normal child development, the sensory world in which we live, common sense, self-respect, respect for other parents and respect and empathy for babies/toddlers.

In my experience, and from what I have observed, parenting is a personal choice and there is no right or wrong way to bring up children. One size does not fit all, and one style of parenting will not suit everyone. My belief and rationale is that parenting should be child-centred, and if baby is happy, then mum, dad and the rest of the family will be happy too.

### Dad's involvement

Fathers are now much more involved in the care of their baby than they were 20 years ago; an increasing number of dads share childcare, or are the primary carer while their wife/partner goes to work. Latest research reported that men were just as attentive and responsive to their baby as women; however, the research noted that, after a few months, fathers were less involved in the care of their baby, and consequently were less responsive to their baby in comparison with the mother. The research concluded that mothers took on the lead parenting role, excluding the father. I was interested to read this research, as this was my observation during professional practice; my thoughts were that fathers became less responsive to their baby's needs when they returned to work, and consequently spent less time getting to know their baby. However, to address the imbalance, I recommended that, where possible, fathers became part of the bedtime routine and spent quality time with their baby.

**Yummy mummy**

Having a new baby means that there are lots of changes and adjustments to make, and lack of sleep compounds the responsibility, stress and anxiety of bringing up children. Many professional women have commented to me that having a baby did not match their expectations and that they felt they had lost their identity. Lack of sleep reduces self-confidence and can increase the risk of post-natal depression. Pressure from the media and celebrity mums has increased the expectation of new mums to become a 'Yummy Mummy' and this increases the pressure on women to be the perfect wife/partner/mother and lose their baby weight within weeks of the birth. For most new mums, this is not realistic and does more harm than good to a woman's self-esteem.

# Attachment Parenting v Babywise Parenting

While researching for this book, I came across an article in *The Journal of Perinatal Education*, 2004 by Barbara Hotelling. At the time, she was president of Lamaze International, and contrasted two current parenting styles: Attachment Parenting (from *Attachment Parenting International*) and Babywise Parenting (from *On Becoming Babywise*) by Garry Ezzo and Robert Bucknam, MD.

**Attachment Parenting**

> "*The theory of Attachment Parenting is it promotes securely attached children. Attachment parenting develops an infant's need for trust, empathy and affection in order to create a secure peaceful and lasting relationship. This style requires a consistent, loving and responsive parent especially during the first 3-5 years of life. The three key elements of Attachment Parenting are bed sharing, breast-feeding, and baby wearing. Attachment Parenting advocates safe bed sharing, only recommended if the parents are non-drug or alcohol users and they sleep on a safe, firm mattress.*"

My Multi-Sensory Approach to sleep can easily be adapted for Attachment Parenting. Although I respect and admire the philosophy of Attachment Parenting, 'bed sharing' and 'baby wearing' does not suit all mothers or babies. From experience, not every baby wants to be cradled in a sling, and not all mums want to sleep with their baby. One mum said her baby hated being in the sling: "*He was just not a cuddly baby.*" Mums I met had safety concerns about 'bed sharing' and preferred 'room sharing' instead.

**Babywise Parenting**

> "*Babywise Parenting is family-centred, not child-centred and regards their baby as a welcome addition to the family but not the centre of the family universe. Feeding, playtime and sleep time are parent-directed and Babywise Parenting claims that parents can establish a routine in their baby's life from day one and stick to it no matter what. When nap-time comes, the baby goes down in the cot and is left to cry until asleep. Babywise claim that leaving a baby to cry everyday for 15-20 minutes is not going to harm your baby, physically or emotionally. Meal times are scheduled and strictly adhered to. If baby does not eat then s/he waits until the next one.*"

My thought on this style of parenting is that it is harsh and does not respect the needs of the baby; my approach to sleep is baby-led. Wait until your baby shows signs of tiredness, and then put your baby down in the cot for a nap. Leaving a baby to cry itself to sleep every day is not recognising that babies are individuals.

### How your baby's personality can affect sleeping patterns

I have identified two personality traits that affect babies' sleep and their ability to learn to self-settle.

### The shy, sensitive baby

If you are a shy, sensitive person, then some of your personality and characteristics are carried in your genes and passed down to your baby; personality traits are hereditary and babies are born with them. If your baby has a sensitive nature and a determined personality trait, resolving a sleep problem can require extra time and patience. My Multi-Sensory Approach to sleep is perfect for sensitive babies: it calms, relaxes and helps babies make positive sleep associations. In my experience, sensitive babies seem more relaxed if they have a structured routine.

Sensitive babies are wary and cautious of new experiences and need time to adapt to changes in their surroundings. When a parent recognises that they have a sensitive baby, they can respond to their baby's needs in the most appropriate empathic way: sensitive babies require more time to adjust to any changes in their life, such as meeting new people, visiting new places and changes of routine. Giving your baby more time to adjust will reduce their stress levels and re-build their confidence and security.

I recommend that you keep your sensitive baby's sleeping environment as stable and controlled as possible. By following my Multi-Sensory Sleep Techniques appropriate for your baby's age, you are gradually introducing your baby to the sensory world.

### Key points for the shy, sensitive baby

- Encourage a positive sleep attachment
- Avoid making any changes that could disrupt the routine
- Avoid starting the sleep routines too early, as resistance, crying and any emotional upset at bedtime are not conducive to relaxation

- Aim to make every sleep time baby-led and not mum-led; in my experience, starting the sleep routine too early causes resistance and is the main cause of sleep problems in older babies

- Incorporate quiet playtime in the nursery before bath time as part of the sleep routine; this will signal to your baby that the bath routine is about to start

- Keep the bath-to-cot/bed sequence short, simple and flowing

- Avoid disruptions, such as going into other rooms to get clothes

- Prepare the nursery before you start the bath routine

- Incorporate a bath every night, as the warm, cosy effect of a bath has a soporific effect, while being aware that it only lasts for 20 minutes

- Keep sleep routines simple, uncomplicated and repetitive, as your sensitive baby will notice any changes

**The adventurous baby**

I have used this expression many times to describe a baby: usually a boy, who is full of fun and energy, 'into everything', fearless and wanting to explore the world. Quite often, they have an independent, determined and persistent streak, which can lead to inner conflict, especially if they have become dependent on their mum to help them to sleep. The older babies become very bossy and demanding at sleep time. My Multi-Sensory Approach to sleep is just what the adventurous baby needs. In my experience, babies who are naturally independent adapt very quickly to self-settling; as soon as they are in control of their sleep and know how to self-settle, sleep problems are a distant memory. Follow a simple, structured sleep routine that is baby-led and not mum-led.

**Key points for the adventurous baby**

- Allow your baby to lead their sleep, but you make the rules and you keep the boundaries
- Introduce your baby to positive sleep associations as they are the key to self-settling
- Very active babies need time to relax and calm down after periods of activity
- As beneficial as they are, day nursery and baby groups can be over-stimulating for some babies, so take time out to de-stress your baby
- Spend quality time together
- Avoid rushing bedtime, and wait until your baby has had enough playtime before starting the bedtime sequence; babies who can relax and self-soothe enjoy sleeping
- Make bedtime the best part of their day

I recommend that you now read the appropriate 'What to Expect' chapter for the age of your baby.

*I hope my children look back on today*
*And see a mother who had time to play*
*There will be years*
*For cleaning and cooking*
*So quiet down cobwebs*
*Dust go to sleep*
*I'm rocking my baby*
*And babies don't keep*

Chapter five

# What to expect in babies from newborn to three months

*"I recommend that new mums spend more time in their bedroom for the first few days."*

After months of waiting, your baby is here at last. It is your first night at home with your new baby; you and your partner are home alone. There are no midwives to offer advice and your head is spinning with all the new experiences and you are feeling very emotional. You have read all 'the books' but none of them can prepare you for the emotional rollercoaster ride ahead. The first night can be terrifying, and there is very little you can do to prepare yourself for it: this is every parent's rite of passage to parenthood. What you can do is make yourself and your new baby very comfortable in your bedroom, play calming, relaxing sleep sounds, dim the lights to a soft glow and make the room a relaxing and calming environment and take your time to bond with your baby and get to know each other.

### How to reduce maternal anxiety

Sleep is such a talked about subject, and every new parent is asked within weeks of the birth, *"Baby sleeping yet?"* How many parents can say, *"Oh, yes, we've been sleeping through since six weeks!"* If you follow my Multi-Sensory Sleep Techniques and Routines, your healthy, full term six- to eight-week-old baby will have the ability to sleep from 11pm until 4 or 5am every night. Sounds too good to be true? Babies need their sleep, and so do mums to recover from the birth. Knowledge is power, and when parents appreciate sleep from their baby's perspective, they realise how to achieve positive sleep associations for their baby; this achievement empowers parents. In my experience, mothers who feel confident about their baby's feeding and sleep patterns are less anxious and worried about their baby. Lack of sleep, not coping, feeling anxious and not being fully in control all contribute towards women developing postnatal depression. My primary objective is to reduce parental anxiety so that every parent can enjoy this amazing time of their lives. I decided to write about my experience of infant sleep and the behavioural problems associated with it.

**In this chapter:**

- Recommended sleeping positions for your newborn
- Multi-sensory techniques for newborn babies
- How much sleep does my baby need?
- How to make positive sleep association for babies
- Bedtime routine
- Frequently asked questions for newborns to three months

## Recommended sleeping positions for your newborn

In the early 1980s, the occurrence of Sudden Infant Death Syndrome (SIDS) was 50% higher than it is today. When TV presenter Ann Diamond's baby died of SIDS, she campaigned for more research on sleeping practices and pioneered the 'back to sleep' campaign. Maternity hospital midwives and health visitors supported the advice, and encouraged parents to change to the 'back to sleep' sleeping position. The results were remarkable; the death rate for SIDS dropped dramatically.

### Research (McNamara 2012) recommends that babies:

- Sleep on their back
- Sleep on a firm, flat mattress designed for babies, i.e. a Moses basket, crib or cot
- Sleep in the parents' room, room-sharing without bed-sharing for six months; room sharing allows the mum to feed, comfort and monitor her baby
- Are breastfed, ideally
- Receive all routine immunisations
- Use a dummy at every sleep time

### It also recommends that babies:

- Do not sleep on soft bedding such as pillows, duvets, chairs or sofas
- Are protected from overheating; babies who like to be swaddled can be safely wrapped in a one-layer swaddling sheet specially designed for babies
- Are not exposed to tobacco smoke, alcohol or illicit drugs

The following background information supports the research findings:

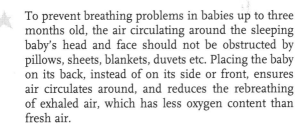

To prevent breathing problems in babies up to three months old, the air circulating around the sleeping baby's head and face should not be obstructed by pillows, sheets, blankets, duvets etc. Placing the baby on its back, instead of on its side or front, ensures air circulates around, and reduces the rebreathing of exhaled air, which has less oxygen content than fresh air.

The research also suggests that when babies use a dummy at sleep time, the action of sucking also prevents breathing problems in babies. However, the research states that using a dummy during the first week of breastfeeding can reduce breastfeeding duration, but not if introduced after one month of exclusive breastfeeding.

## Settling your new baby into their sleeping area

I recommend that new mums spend more time in their bedroom for the first few days, to aid recovery from the delivery and to make the most of this special time to bond with their baby. Babies have short memories, and sleep better if they sleep in the same place during the day and night.

## Sleeping places to avoid

Avoid letting your baby sleep in a baby chair or car seat for long periods. Ideally, babies should lie flat during their sleep, as they have more room to stretch, kick and move about. I have visited babies that would only sleep in the car seat during the night. Many of these were babies with a diagnosis of Gastro Oesophageal Reflex (GOR). However, there are special wedges designed for cots that are often recommended to relieve the symptoms of GOR. More information and tips about GOR are contained in Chapter 14.

I guarantee that strong odours and cooking smells will waken your sleeping baby and stimulate their instinct to root for milk. I recommend that you move your baby away from cooking smells so that you can enjoy your meal in peace. Newborn babies are also sensitive to sudden noise and can become overstimulated by constant loud noises; noise sensitivity occurs in busy households with noisy young children. However, babies do not like it to be completely quiet either. The low rumble of familiar sounds, your voice and familiar music are reassuring and comforting for babies.

## Baby wearing

Slings are practical and a great way to soothe and calm wakeful, restless and unsettled babies. However, if you have had a C-section, physiotherapists recommend waiting six weeks before wearing one. The advantages of wearing a sling or, as some mums call it, 'baby wearing', are that your hands are free and your baby is close to you. 'Slinging' your baby helps to comfort babies with GOR and colic (see frequently asked questions at the end of this chapter). However, do not assume that your baby will enjoy a sling; I have heard mums say that their baby did not like being in the sling. This highlights the fact that babies are individuals, born

Ewan the Dream Sheep (left) plays womb sounds ideal newborn babies

with personality, likes and dislikes, and not every baby is a 'cuddly baby'. Most towns have a Sling Library, which offers the option to 'try before you buy'. The library will also have a consultant who can advise on wearing a sling.

Whilst in the womb, your baby has been used to a confined space, and this is why most babies like swaddling and cuddling; there are special wraps designed to swaddle babies safely and make a positive sleep association. Mothers who 'sling' and 'co-sleep' with their babies are making the child feel safe and secure (see Attachment Parenting in chapter four).

## Moses basket versus cot

Many parents will have chosen a Moses basket or crib before the birth, as they are small, portable and look lovely, but most babies outgrow them within weeks of birth. As soon as your baby can touch the sides of the Moses basket, it is time to move him to a cot. Parents worry that their baby is too small for a cot, yet often the baby is sleeping in their double/king sized bed. I have found babies sleep much better in their cot as they can stretch out and kick freely, and when they are asleep they look so relaxed.

If you cannot fit a large cot into your bedroom, there are smaller cots that will fit most rooms, but some parents have no choice and have to set up the cot in the nursery. Make the transition as easy as possible for your baby: spend time in the nursery, sit and read stories; babies love the sound of your voice. Attach a battery operated mobile to the cot: the Fisher Price Rainforest mobile is very popular (see picture in chapter three). Entertain and play with your baby while they lie in the cot; even very young babies like gazing up at the mobile. To help with the transition from Moses basket to cot, place the Moses basket in the cot and let your baby sleep in there during the day. Using the nursery will ensure that it becomes a familiar peaceful place for your baby. For your own peace of mind, set up a baby monitor with a camera.

## Newborn babies and family bonding

Cradling, feeding, changing, dressing, bathing and talking to your baby is a bonding experience for both parents and baby. Babies bond with their primary carer, the person that gives them the most care and attention; therefore, it is important that only significant people are involved in your baby's care. Several years ago, I met Janis, a busy third-time mum. Janis was very grateful for help with her newborn baby; aunts, friends and older siblings were involved in his care, bathing, changing and feeding him. After a few weeks, Janis noticed that he cried every time she picked him up; she was very upset that he did not seem to know her as his mum; she realised that this was because she was not feeding or changing him during the day. This was a shock to Janis, as she had not realised her baby was so sensitive and aware of his environment, or that he could make attachments to other members of her family.

Fortunately, within days she had resolved the problem; by carrying out all feeding, changing and bathing, she became his mum again.

Everyone wants to meet the new arrival, and often the first weeks are hectic with visiting family and friends. I recommend that, once the immediate family have bonded with the baby, introduce other family members at your pace and your baby's pace. Too many new experiences, changes of environment and prolonged contacts will overtire you and overstimulate your baby. Babies are very sensitive to lots of attention and can be unsettled for several days afterwards. Most mums said that it took until the following Wednesday for their baby to settle back into their routine after a busy weekend. Never underestimate how sensitive your baby is to change in routine. Some take longer to adapt to new experiences than others. Your baby's personality will determine how he/she reacts to change.

# Multi-sensory techniques for newborn babies

Here are some tips to make your baby's sleeping environment conducive to sleep and relaxation:

 The bedroom where your baby sleeps at night should feel relaxing, calming and peaceful; it is an important place for you and your baby, so create a sensory sleeping environment from day one.

 Make some space near your bed for the Moses basket or crib; I recommend a non-rocking crib, as the rocking motion can disturb babies if they move about in their sleep.

 The bedroom should have a strong visual focal point; as babies gaze intently at lights, position a soft, glowing night light where your baby can gaze at it while they are in the Moses basket; choose a night light that you can transfer to the nursery later.

- Introduce your baby to a comforter impregnated with your personal scent; keep the comforter down your top while you feed your baby.

- Leave your baby's bedding under your duvet for a few hours.

- You can opt to introduce a sleep toy such as Ewan the Dream sheep; it plays womb sounds and has a soft, red glow light that attracts a young baby's attention. Make room for a comfortable chair in which to feed and cuddle your baby.

# How much sleep does my baby need?

The following are my observations of normal, healthy, full term babies, collated over 30 years (read more about sleep in chapter one):

- The average amount of sleep babies have in 24 hours is 12-14 hours; each baby has their own unique age related sleep potential and, no matter how hard you try, you cannot increase the number of hours your baby sleeps in any 24 hour period.

- Sleep studies have measured baby sleep cycles, and newborn babies spend 90% of their sleep in REM, light dreaming sleep.

**The typical sleep pattern for a two- to six-week-old baby**

During the day, babies are awake, on average, for one to two hours at a time, and asleep for two to three hours at a time. Wake your baby after a three-hour daytime sleep, as prolonged day sleeps will shorten night sleep, and it interferes with feeding patterns. Most babies start their night sleep from 11pm to midnight, and will sleep for a block of four hours without waking.

**The typical sleep pattern for a three-month-old baby**

Your baby's sleeping pattern changes weekly, and as each week goes by, your baby will sleep longer at night. During the day, they are more active between feeds and stay awake for longer, playing and looking around. Some babies, but not all, can have enough energy to stay awake for two to three hours at a time. Avoid 'mum managing' your baby's sleep, for example, by rocking and feeding them to sleep; babies will sleep when they are ready. Take your tired baby to their nursery for quiet sensory play time and if they are ready for sleep, they will be relaxed enough to drift off naturally with minimum intervention.

At three months of age, most babies are ready for bedtime at 8pm. If babies are good at settling to sleep and able to self-settle at bedtime, most have the potential to sleep for six to eight hours without waking, and the only thing that wakes them is hunger. There are three changes in their sleep cycles:

- Between 8pm and 11pm, they are in REM sleep, are often very restless and wake up
- Between midnight and 4am, they are in peaceful Non-REM sleep
- Between 4am and 7am, they are back in REM sleep, and wake up every two hours until morning

## How to make positive sleep associations for babies

Babies use all five senses – smell, sound, sight, touch and taste – from the moment they are born and from the moment you arrive home from hospital, your newborn will be processing everything around him using all his senses. Your baby will rapidly become familiar with the world and within days of birth, your smell, touch and your voice are imprinted into your baby's brain.

The senses are in the same area of the brain as memory and emotion and is the reason why the senses are so evocative and trigger memories from years gone by. Each sense has an association with sleep. For example, if your baby falls asleep while being cradled or fed, you will become your baby's sleep association. Each sense is activated: your smell, your touch, the taste of your milk, the sound of your voice, your heartbeat and the sight of your face. You are your baby's sleep association, and only you will be able to settle your baby to sleep.

Your baby can make positive sleep associations to a teddy/comforter, a soft, glowing night light and relaxing nature sounds. Babies make sleep associations with all five senses. It is best to introduce your baby to positive sleep attachments and sleep associations from birth. Introducing positive sleep associations to newborns does not involve 'training' your baby in any way. My Multi-Sensory Approach to sleep will encourage your baby to self-soothe, which enables them to reach their maximum age related sleep potential.

It is possible for very young babies to make positive sleep associations independent from you. From newborn, you can encourage your baby to make sleep attachments to a comforter with your scent (smell), a soft teddy (touch), soft, glowing light (sight), nature sounds or heartbeat (sound) or a dummy (taste). This is how you do it:

## Smell

Babies can recognise the smell of their mother's milk within days of birth. Using this amazing fact to your advantage: scent a comforter within your bra whilst breastfeeding as this will give your baby the opportunity to smell and touch the comforter while they feed. Attach the comforter safely to the Moses basket so that your baby can smell it at sleep times; the smell of the comforter will quickly become a positive sleep-smell association, will soothe your baby and be a comforting and familiar reminder of you. A comforter can become a very positive sleep association and will aid self-settling. Give it to your baby at every sleep time. It is a good idea to have a few, just in case you lose one.

# Sight

From birth, your baby can focus on objects at a distance of six to eight inches, which is the distance between you and your baby when your baby is breastfeeding or being cuddled. Babies look at faces more than any other shape. They also stare at lights, black and white shapes, and bright primary colours: red, yellow and blue.

I recommend using a battery operated cot mobile from four to six weeks, as it develops eye coordination and entertains your baby while in the cot. (See the Rainforest Mobile pictured in chapter three.)

Using a night lamp that changes colour will create an interesting visual focus at sleep times and will become a relaxing, positive sleep association. Take the lamp into the nursery when your baby is ready to make the transition from your room to the nursery. One couple told me about their experiences of lights: they could not understand why their baby was unable to settle in the nursery, as he had slept so well in their bedroom; then they remembered that their baby liked to stare at the soft-glow decorative lights in their bedroom. As soon as they brought the lights into the nursery, he turned to look at them and continued to gaze at them before drifting off to sleep! A strong visual focus at sleep time will become a positive sleep association and I recommend that parents use a portable sleep toy, such as a Slumber Buddy, which has a variety of light options.

# Sound

The first sounds your baby hears are womb sounds, your heartbeat and your voice. From birth, they are familiar and comforting, and many mums notice that their baby stops crying in response to their voice. I have noticed that babies will gravitate to the left side of your chest to listen and feel your heartbeat. Sleep toys that replicate the sound of the heartbeat are available; if used at every sleep time, your baby will relax, self-settle and make a positive sleep association with the sleep toy. New babies respond very well to heartbeat, but older babies lose interest and develop a preference for other sounds; Ewan the Dream Sheep is very popular with newborn babies.

## Classical music

Talking and singing to your baby is relaxing and soothing. I know many mums play music to their babies whilst in the womb, and playing the same music has a calming effect on their newborn baby. I recommend that mums use the same music in the bedroom at sleep time, as it has already become a positive sleep association. If your baby does not appear to react in a positive way to music, introduce one piece of soothing music of your choice and make it part of the bedroom/nursery experience. Babies like classical music that has 60 beats per minute; the beat is repetitive and reminds the baby of your heartbeat. They also respond well to ocean/sea sounds as they are very relaxing and hypnotic.

## Nature sounds

I have noticed that babies like ocean and nature sounds, jungle noises and garden bird song. A mum from Finland told me that it was common practice to leave babies in their prams to sleep outside in the garden. She had been following that practice with Fleur, her four-month-old baby, during the day and could not understand why she had problems with her baby settling at bedtime. To replicate the garden experience, we used a Slumber Buddy which played the sound of garden birds and when Fleur heard it, she immediately stopped crying, relaxed and drifted off to sleep. Never underestimate the power of a sleep-sound association; once you know what helps your baby to relax, chill and drift off to sleep, you will make it part of the settling sequence. However, once your baby is asleep switch off all sound; otherwise, it will permeate into your baby's subconscious mind and your baby will become reliant on it to sustain sleep.

# Touch

Mother and baby skin-to-skin contact is a wonderful experience and produces endorphins in both. Breastfed babies will knead and stroke their mum's breast and clothes – a perfect situation to begin a sleep-touch association.

### Replicate cuddles at sleep time

New babies love to be held and cuddled, but although close physical contact is very important during waking hours, babies do not need cuddles during sleep. It is natural to hold a newborn baby until he has gone to sleep, but once asleep, let your baby finish his sleep in the Moses basket, preferably in the room he will sleep in at night.

### Startle reflex

If the startle reflex wakens your baby, try this technique and repeat it every sleep time until your baby is used to sleeping in the Moses basket:

- Turn your baby slightly to one side
- Place a very soft ten-inch teddy behind your baby
- Place the scented comforter close enough so that your baby can feel the softness on his cheek
- If the baby is wriggly, gently hold his hands and stroke his face; do this until your baby relaxes and drifts off to sleep

**Important note:** To comply with safe sleeping recommendations, do not leave your baby in this position, as soon as your baby is asleep:

- Remove the teddy
- Attach the comforter to the Moses basket
- Turn your baby onto his back

# Taste

It is normal for babies from birth to six weeks to fall asleep whilst being fed. However, after six weeks, this changes and babies are more awake between feeds and stay awake for longer. Always aim to feed your baby after a sleep, not before, to ensure that your baby is eager and ready to feed; it also prevents sleepy feeds, and your baby falling asleep halfway through a feed. I have noticed that alert babies feed more vigorously, their sucking action is stronger and this increases the production of the breast-milk hormone, prolactin. Conversely, babies who fall asleep within minutes of breastfeeding are snack feeding and consequentially appear constantly tired and hungry.

# Bedtime routine

One of the key elements to settling healthy, full term babies, is realising that their sleeping pattern is identical to the one before birth. If you could feel your unborn baby moving about in the evening, this is the wake/sleep pattern they will have until they are two weeks old. Most 'evening' babies are restless, cluster feed and catnap until midnight.

**When your baby is six weeks old commence this routine:**

1   Start the bedtime routine from 10pm.

2   Take your baby up to the bedroom and start the settling process with soft glow lights and any soothing sleep music.

3   Avoid watching the TV in the bedroom, or using your mobile phone or computer; it is distracting and not conducive for sleep; this is a time to relax and settle your baby ready for sleep.

4   Begin the bedtime routine with a milk feed followed by a bath, or just a top to toe.

5   Cradle your baby for a few minutes, until relaxed but not asleep and then put your baby into the cot. Use a soft red light, a soothing sleep sound such as waves or heart beat, and stroke your baby's face nose and mouth with a comforter until they are asleep. This is the quickest way to make a sleep association with a teddy or comforter.

   Ewan the dream sheep has an ideal light and sleep sound for this age group.

6   Babies have a naturally strong urge to suck. If you feel your baby would settle more easily with a dummy use one for a few months.

7  Very often, babies rouse when they are put in the cot. If this happens, follow the procedure for startle reflex on the previous page.

8  If your baby has a dummy, remove it after a few minutes of sleep, as this reduces dependency upon it and stops the dummy becoming a habit. A dummy is not recommended for breastfed babies until breastfeeding has been established, normally at about four to six weeks after birth.

9  Turn off the music and lights as soon as your baby is asleep.

10  When baby wakes in the night, feed in dim light, in a comfortable chair and when your baby has finished feeding, put him back in the Moses basket.

## Problems with day naps

Up until six weeks old most babies will sleep anywhere and are not aware of their surroundings. It is during this period that parents notice that, once asleep, nothing usually disturbs their baby. This can cause parents to have a false sense of security as after six weeks it is a totally different story. Babies are more awake and alert, taking notice of everything around them and some babies cry if taken to new environments. The noise levels and smells in some shops, coffee shops and restaurants are excessively high and babies are over-stimulated by loud noise, strong smells and easily woken from light sleep. It is from this age that mums start to develop a technique that settles baby to sleep, either with a feed, a rock or a cuddle. If you would prefer your baby to sleep more independently, here is the perfect routine for you.

### Daytime nap routine from six weeks old

1  Aim to have at least one, if not all, daytime naps in the cot. Use the same sensory attachments such as Ewan the Dream Sheep or the Slumber Buddy and a comforter that smells of you.

2  To reinforce a positive association with the cot, basket or crib, ensure your baby has a couple of play sessions in there every day. These play sessions are not part of the sleep routine. They are fun, multi-sensory and the Fisher Price rainforest mobile is an ideal contribution to sensory playtime. Babies have very short attention spans therefore playtime may only last three to four minutes.

3  When your baby has been awake for a while and is showing all the tired signs take your baby up to their bedroom.

4  Put your baby in the cot and switch on the mobile. At this stage wait to see what your baby wants to do. Some babies still want to play, in which case show your baby more toys and rattles.

5  As soon as your baby has lost interest in toys, and starts to cry, close the curtains, switch off the mobile, turn on the red light and sleep sound, stroke your baby's face, nose and mouth with the scented comforter. Do that at every sleep time and your baby will develop a sleep attachment to a teddy or comforter. Talk to your baby and tell them how tired they are, this is better than "shushing".

6  When your baby has relaxed into sleep turn off the red light and sleep sound, attach the comforter to the cot and remove the teddies.

# Frequently asked questions for newborns to three months

### Q. What is colic?

**A.** Babies bowels are extremely active. Milk is constantly being digested and the waste product of milk produces lots of gas and wind. Babies with feeding problems such as constipation, allergies to cows milk or milk intolerance produce more wind than is comfortable for babies and the pressure in the bowel causes increased discomfort and pain. Many babies are given the term 'evening colic' to describe their crying in the evening. Every evening at around 6 pm, they start to have bouts of inconsolable crying. The pain of colic and the cry of an overtired, irritable baby can seem identical. When babies cry, they screw up their faces, look red in the face and move their arms and legs about in a very agitated way. Babies with 'evening colic' are often babies with sensitive personalities. Their colic can be relieved with a warm, deep bath and abdominal baby massage. My Multi-Sensory Sleep Techniques help to distract, settle and soothe babies with colic. Fortunately 'evening colic' resolves itself without treatment by three to four months of age.

### Q. Should I worry about leaving my new baby to sleep in my bedroom during the day?

**A.** It is very natural to be worried when you first leave your newborn to sleep on his own. However, the lounge environment is too stimulating for most babies, and it is not a practical place to leave a baby to sleep, with or without inquisitive toddlers or pets around. Also, it is important that babies should make a positive sleep association with the room they sleep in at night. Play soothing sleep music in the bedroom to encourage a positive sleep-sound association. Scent a comforter with your scent and leave it with your baby while he sleeps. To help ease your worry and anxiety about leaving your baby, use a baby monitor that has a camera, so that your baby can sleep in peace and you have peace of mind.

### Q. My six-week-old baby has evening colic and prefers to sleep on my chest. He cries if I put him down in the Moses basket. What can I do about this?

**A.** Babies with colic and reflux are fussy, irritable babies and parents will do anything to settle their distressed baby. However, by the time they are six months old, most babies have outgrown colic and reflux, but are still sleeping on mum or dad; they now have a sleeping problem caused by colic and reflux. The first thing to do is to obtain the correct diagnosis and treatment. Consult your GP, and once you have started treatment, start to implement my Multi-Sensory Techniques. The Multi-Sensory Sleep Approach is perfect for colicky babies. Introduce a comforter so that your baby can make an attachment to it; soft glow and interesting lights will distract your baby from crying. Playing soothing sleep music will relax and calm your baby.

### Q. My baby is three weeks old, but I want to be flexible and give my baby some of my expressed milk in a bottle. When is the best time to introduce this technique?

**A.** If you are a new mum, don't start expressing until your baby is four weeks old, to ensure that breastfeeding is established and you are feeling confident about it. The best time to express your milk is after the first feed in the morning, between 6am and 8am. Use a manual, battery operated or electric breast pump, save the milk in the fridge and either use it within two to three days, or freeze it on the same day that it was expressed. Breastfed babies like a soft teat, so choose a brand that specialises in a breast/bottle style. The best time to give a breastfed baby a bottle of warmed, expressed milk is in the evening, anytime from 8-11pm. This is a good time for dads to be involved in the feeding. Breastfeed during the night after you have had some sleep, as the prolactin levels are highest after deep sleep, milk production is good and your baby will have a good feed.

### Q. My three-month-old baby will only go to sleep if I breastfeed her. How can I stop this?

**A.** Three-month-old babies who only fall asleep during a feed have developed a milk-sleep association. This is very habit forming, and as babies get older they become more dependent on breast milk to settle to sleep. The easiest way to stop this happening is teach your baby to self-settle without breastfeeding by following my Multi-Sensory Sleep Techniques for breastfed babies. Settle your baby to sleep without feeding, routinely give a breastfeed when your baby wakes up from a nap and give the last feed in the lounge, before the bath, as this prevents a milk-sleep association. If you are able to achieve this, hunger will naturally wake your baby.

### Q. At what age should my baby sleep through the night without needing a milk feed?

**A.** Most healthy, full term, two-month-old, breast or bottle fed babies have the potential to sleep from 11pm until 4-6am, or five to seven hours, without waking for milk. However, this average applies only to babies who can self-settle and have made positive sleep attachments.

**Q. At what age can my baby go into a cot?**

**A.** Babies can go into a cot from birth. However, most parents prefer to use a Moses basket or a crib for a few months, as they fit easily into the parents' bedroom. The ideal time to use a cot is from three months, as by then most babies are too big for the Moses basket and can touch the sides of the cot and wake themselves up. This is also an opportunity to use a battery operated mobile attached to the cot, as it encourages eye coordination and entertains babies until they are ready to go to sleep.

**Q. My baby is 11 weeks old, is still sleeping in the Moses basket and has started to wake up in the night. Is she hungry?**

**A.** Babies of 11 weeks who wake up in the night have outgrown the Moses basket. Babies grow very quickly and when they can touch the sides of the Moses basket the action disturbs their sleep. Once awake, babies want milk to go back to sleep. Start to use a cot now and you will see how comfortable your baby looks, and will notice a huge difference in your baby's sleep.

**Q. My baby is three months old and too big for the Moses basket, but I don't have space in my bedroom for a cot. I have read that babies should sleep with their mums for six months. What should I do?**

**A.** The average sized Moses basket is too small for babies over 12 lbs. So the dilemma is: where is the safest place for baby to sleep? Cot beds are too big for the average bedroom, so decide where you want your baby to sleep. A small cot or crib would fit into most parents' bedroom, but if that is not an option for you, then a cot in the nursery is the safest place for baby to sleep. Place baby at the foot of the cot in a sleeping bag, and set up a baby listening monitor to give you reassurance.

# Chapter six

# What to expect in babies aged three to six months

*"Whatever your baby sees, hears, smells, feels and tastes as he drifts off to sleep will become a sleep association."*

This is the age when I noticed that most mums start to settle into motherhood and really enjoy their baby. Babies aged three to six months are happy, vocal babies, who smile at everyone and enjoy simple everyday routines. Mums can recognise their baby's different cries and anticipate what their babies need; learning about your baby's cry is a great confidence booster and lessens maternal anxiety and worry. Going out and meeting other new mums helps with this process too. By three months, breastfeeding is well established and most colic and feeding problems have usually been resolved. Small, subtle, but significant patterns of behaviour will have developed, i.e. the way you hold and interact with your baby, where and how you feed your baby. As the weeks and months go by, these little routines and patterns of behaviour will become a habit and your baby will remember the sequence and action of what you are doing and become excited in anticipation of being fed. Both parents develop their own repetitive way of interacting with their baby; consequently, their baby learns sequences and anticipates what comes next.

**In this chapter:**
- Why do sleep problems occur from age three months
- Multi-sensory sleep techniques
- Day nap routine, three to six months
- Bedtime routine
- What to do if your baby resists and cries
- How to solve a sleep problem

### Why do sleeping problems occur from age three months?

Every day your baby is discovering and learning about his environment using all his five senses. Learning new experiences increases his memory and from three months of age your baby's brain is more able to:

- Process information
- Recognise significant people in their daily life
- Remember and anticipate the sequence of simple daily routines
- Make sleep associations
- Develop preferences, such as the position they sleep in, where they sleep and how they like to be held and fed

Whatever your baby sees, hears, smells, feels and tastes as he drifts off to sleep will become a sleep association. If it is a positive sleep association, your baby will sleep to his unique age related sleep potential, but if it is negative, your baby will wake up frequently throughout the night.

### Existing sleep associations

*"What has happened? My baby used to sleep through but now wakes three to four times a night."* So many parents contact me about this problem, wondering what has changed as their baby was sleeping so well. The simple answer is, their baby is more aware

of what is going on around them and has started to make sleep attachments and sleep associations. Without exception, babies that are fed to sleep, use a dummy at sleep times, or are rocked/patted/shushed to sleep, have developed negative sleep associations and will wake frequently during the night. Babies who can self-settle without parental involvement or intervention sleep through to their maximum age related sleep potential.

### Age related sleep potential

By the age of three months, most babies are capable of sleeping for six to eight hours at night without waking for a milk feed. The average number of hours a baby will sleep in a whole day is 12-14. However, every baby is unique and some babies only sleep for 11 hours in a 24 hour period. Daytime naps are important for babies and most have one or two hours of sleep a day, but this can vary depending on your baby's activity levels during the day. (See chapter one for more about sleep patterns.)

# Multi-sensory sleep techniques

Now is a good time to introduce positive sleep attachments such as a teddy/comforter, soft glowing night light and soothing nature sounds.

### Vision

By age four months, your baby has perfect vision and can focus on any moving object. The sense of sight is situated in the same area of the brain as memory and emotion; clear, perfect vision stimulates this area of the brain and babies can recognise familiar objects. Three-month-old babies will watch their mother intently as she moves about a room. If you have not already done so, introduce a morphing colourful night light. It will become a sleep association and make the bedroom relaxing and calming. A soft, red glow is more relaxing just before sleep than white, green or blue lights. However, light shows will attract your baby's attention and keep your baby amused until he is ready to sleep. Cot mobiles develop eye coordination and help to keep babies happy and amused while they lie in the cot. A pleasurable experience in the cot will create a positive association with it.

### Touch

From four months of age, babies are naturally inquisitive and learn to reach out, grasping for objects within their reach and taking them to their mouths. Babies learn about the object by feeling it and tasting it. Babies who fall asleep at the breast have developed a strong sleep/touch/taste attachment to the breast and nipple. I have observed babies touch, stroke and knead their mum's breast and clothing during a feed; this is how attachments to a scarf, clothes labels or feeding muslins originate. Now is a good time to introduce a comforter: place a comforter (a soft cloth blanket 10 x 10 inches) down your bra when you feed. This will enable your baby to hold and stroke the soft comforter as he feeds and he will make a positive association with the comforter as it has been impregnated with your scent; if it is given to your baby at every sleep time, it will become a positive sleep association. This is such a simple, but effective, step to take and it makes such a huge impact on how long your baby will sleep for during the night. Mums who 'bed share' can still use comforters for their baby and it makes the transition from mum's bed to the cot, and from cot to bed, so much easier. Cuddle your baby with two soft 10-12 inch teddies, and your baby will feel very secure and they could become 'best friends'.

### Sound

Language development escalates from three months onwards. Babies focus very intently on their mum's face and communicate with lots of vocalisation: cooing, 'agoo', 'agee' and 'ooo' sounds. Babies will watch their mother's face during one-to-one social interactions and even take turns with 'goos' and 'oos' as if they are having a real conversation. Babies love listening to your voice. To encourage a positive sleep association with their cot, tell stories or sing while they lie in it; add some nature sounds and you will have created the perfect sensory environment for positive sleep-sound association.

## Taste

All newborn babies have a strong desire to suck the breast, bottle or dummy, but by six months they lose interest in sucking and start to chew, sip and swallow in preparation for weaning. If babies have been fed to sleep they have developed a milk-sleep association. To stop this occurring, avoid sleepy/comfort feeds and aim to feed your baby after a day nap rather than before a nap; your baby will be more alert and feed so much better. Follow the Multi-Sensory Sleep Routine and give the last milk feed in the lounge before the bath.

Dummies are very addictive and babies who have a dummy in their mouth all the time develop a taste-sleep association and, ultimately, a sleeping problem. Typically, the dummy falls out of their mouth during sleep and the baby wakes up during a light sleep cycle and cries for the dummy; this can happen three or four times a night. To prevent the dummy causing a sleep problem, reduce your baby's dependency on the dummy during the day. Restrict its usage to sleep times only, and do not put the dummy back in straight away. Wait a few minutes to see if your baby can settle without it. As soon as your baby is asleep, remove it from his mouth. During the night, avoid rushing to pop the dummy back in – wait a few minutes. After a few days, increase the time you wait before giving your baby the dummy. Mums who persevered with this approach were able to stop using the dummy within a week. One mum realised that the dummy was a barrier to their mum/baby communication and when she stopped using the dummy, she spent more time finding out what her baby's cries meant and, ultimately, what her baby wanted. The same applies for breastfed babies. Every time a breastfed baby cries, it does not mean the baby needs to be fed.

## Sleeping position

By age three months, full term babies have outgrown Moses baskets and cribs and most are sleeping comfortably in a cot. If your baby is still sleeping in your bedroom, create an area in your bedroom that is just for your baby, separate from yours. If the cot is too big for your bedroom, set up the cot in the nursery and use a baby monitor with a camera. In my experience, babies sleep much better in their own room. You can control the nursery environment and keep the ambience stable, as babies are easily roused in REM sleep, which occurs before midnight and after 4am. There is a lot of advice about babies' sleeping positions: as previously mentioned, guidelines recommend babies sleep on their back; however, in my experience, breastfed babies prefer sleeping on their side. If you are worried, there are special sleeping mattresses designed for side-sleeping, which prevent babies rolling onto their tummies while they are sleep. From six months onwards, many babies prefer to sleep on their side or their tummy and your baby's sleeping position is less of a concern when your baby can roll over. Babies of this age are physically very active and move about using a variety of manoeuvres; some babies can roll onto their tummy and prefer that sleeping position. This is a good age to introduce 'tummy time', which will strengthen neck and shoulder muscles, enabling babies to lift their head and shoulders off the mattress.

**Baby-led sleep**

If your baby is tired, your sleep routine will be successful. Starting the bedtime routine too soon is the number one cause of behavioural problems associated with sleep. If you start to feed to sleep, rock, shush and pat your baby to sleep, I can predict that this will result in a long-term sleeping problem. I know some mums spend hours rocking/patting their baby to sleep and I have witnessed babies become hysterical with temper using this sleeping technique. Your baby might eventually go to sleep, but it will have been an unpleasant power battle for you both. All sleep problems can be avoided; learn to read your baby's tired signs. Yawning is not a true indication of tiredness, babies will yawn when they are bored and to increase oxygen into their lungs; they can trick you into thinking they are tired when they are just bored. Look for more signs, such as crying while rubbing the face or eyes, accompanied by several yawns. Move your baby to another room or show them a different toy and if your baby can perk up, they are not ready for the sleep routine.

# Day nap routine, three to six months, also for babies up to 12 months

## Introducing the cot for day naps

Create a positive sleep association with the cot and make it a fun place to be, let your baby play in there with their favourite toys any time during the day. Treat the cot like a playpen and fill with lots of toys.

If you would like your baby to learn quickly how to sleep peacefully and without resistance, make time to spend two or three days at home for all day naps. Believe me, it is the quickest and easiest way to get your baby sleeping in the cot. This truly is the best investment of your time and makes all the difference. Day naps are the cornerstone of my self-settling techniques. Babies that nap easily in the cot during the day, naturally sleep well at night.

All sleep should be baby led and at three months of age some babies can stay awake for three hours. Older babies can have the energy to stay awake for six hours. Bored babies can trick mum into thinking they are tired but will resist sleep vehemently with screams, hysterics and breath-holding behaviour. Prevent this from happening and only put your baby down for a nap when they are super tired with lots of yawning, rubbing their eyes and a tired cry.

## Cot day nap, day one

 Calculate how long your baby is normally awake for and add on an extra hour. It is important to do this to avoid your baby fighting their sleep. In my experience mums underestimate how long their baby can stay awake for. Babies are very resilient and if given plenty of toys to occupy their mind they can keep going like a Duracell bunny! This technique is baby led sleep, not mum managed sleep.

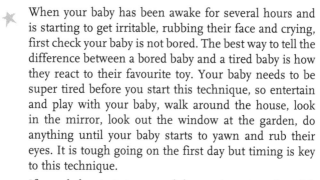

When your baby has been awake for several hours and is starting to get irritable, rubbing their face and crying, first check your baby is not bored. The best way to tell the difference between a bored baby and a tired baby is how they react to their favourite toy. Your baby needs to be super tired before you start this technique, so entertain and play with your baby, walk around the house, look in the mirror, look out the window at the garden, do anything until your baby starts to yawn and rub their eyes. It is tough going on the first day but timing is key to this technique.

If your baby starts to cry and does not want to play with their favourite toy, then yes, they are tired and ready to nap. Now is the time to start the daytime routine.

## Daytime routine, day one

Take your baby to the nursery and just sit your baby on your knee facing outwards.

Slip a thin flat pillow behind your baby's back. This will give your baby something to lean against and act as a barrier between you and your baby. Doing this also prevents your baby arching their back to reach the breast if they are a breastfed baby. Give your baby their comforter/teddy to hold. If your baby has a dummy avoid using it at this stage. If your baby is too wriggly, sit together on a beanbag.

Position a mirror in front of you so you can see what your baby is doing. To create a soothing and relaxing atmosphere, use the red light from the Slumber Buddy and soothing heartbeat sound.

Talk quietly to your baby, and read stories such as *That's not my puppy*, by Fiona Watt. Keep your body steady and avoid any rocking motion.

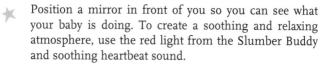

Hold your position and keep steady and calm until you see your baby's eyes are starting to droop.

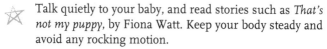

Now close the curtains, put your baby in the cot, and switch on the red light and sleep sound and give your baby their comforter to smell and hold. If your baby is crawling and pulling to stand let your baby walk about the cot. Remove obstructions and obstacles to prevent your baby tripping over them. Gently lie your baby down but he might pull to stand four to five times before being ready to lie down and go to sleep.

If your baby has a frustrated angry cry, respond with: *"you're so tired, come on sleepy baby, sleepy time"*, and repeat this every time your baby cries loudly, tapping the Slumber Buddy shell to attract his attention. Keep stroking your baby's face, nose and mouth with the teddy comforter until asleep. If your baby reaches out for you, hand your baby different teddies, and animate the teddies: *"teddies are so tired, lie down with the teddies"*.

This is the perfect time to allow your baby a few minutes of tired baby cry. If your baby has a dummy wait four to five minutes before you give your baby their dummy. Depending on your baby's personality this tired baby cry can last for five to ten minutes or longer. Older babies like to sleep on their tummy or side. If your baby is used to sleeping on you let your baby sleep sitting up, leaning on a pillow.

As soon as your baby is asleep turn off the red light and sleep sound. Remove toys, place the comforter in his hand and leave the room.

If your timing is right this should only take 20 to 30 minutes the first time. Depending on the baby's personality some babies take longer to sleep on the first attempt. If baby wriggles and squirms and the cry escalates to a hysterical cry after ten minutes, your baby is not tired enough to do this yet, so abandon and try again in an hour's time. At that point you say to yourself: *"okay you're not tired enough, I will play with you, but when you are ready, you are going to sleep in your cot"*, keep positive and calm, sleep will come and your baby can learn to sleep in the cot.

If your baby wakes after 10 to 15 minutes feeling tired, grumpy and miserable, this is because it was a new experience and your baby needs more practice. Do not attempt to resettle your baby as this nap time is over, there will be another nap later. Take your baby out of the room into another environment and wait for your baby to cheer up. The next nap will be easier. Just keep practising. Each time you repeat this your baby's body relaxes and adjusts to sleeping longer in the cot. This technique requires timing, perseverance and repetition and within two to three days' time your baby will have reached their optimum nap time.

**Day nap day two**

Repeat the same routine as day one. You will be able to identify your baby's tired signs and your baby should settle with less resistance. It is still too early to identify a pattern as this will emerge in the next few days.

**Cot day nap day three**

Change the routine today. Instead of sitting your baby on your knee put your baby straight into the cot. Still look out for the tired signs and check your baby isn't bored. You might notice that your baby can stay awake for longer between the naps. Mid-morning and mid-afternoon are ideal for babies having two naps a day. If your baby has an hour-long nap in the afternoon, the nap will keep their battery charged until bedtime.

It is rare for babies under one year old to have one nap a day but not unheard of, and if you have one of those babies an hour-long nap after lunch is ideal.

- Take your baby up to the cot for some daytime playtime, this will test how tired your baby is.

- Keep the curtains open and switch on the mobile, entertain and give your baby toys to play with. Plastic tubs filled with colourful clothes pegs and clips are very entertaining for babies that can sit up.

- If you are sure your baby is tired, keep your baby in the cot and proceed to the nap.

- Close the curtains and switch on the sleep light and sleep sound and give your baby their comforter.

- Stand back from the cot and avoid leaning over and touching as this interrupts their self-settling process.

* If there is resistance and a tired baby cry, stroke their face, nose and mouth with the comforter and talk to your baby.

* When your baby is asleep switch off the light and sleep sound and leave your baby with a comforter in their hand.

**Cot day nap days four to seven**

By the seventh day a regular sleep pattern will have emerged and your baby will sleep peacefully without any crying or resistance. I recommend that your baby has one cot day nap every day to reinforce a positive attachment to the cot.

## Bedtime routine

Babies sleep better if they have a repetitive routine. They have short memories and do not remember events from one day to the next. Set up the nursery and make it 'womb like with stars', a special place to relax, play and sleep. Start the sleep sequence one hour before your baby is normally asleep.

The following is the sequence for babies who are asleep by 8pm. Make sure your baby has had an afternoon nap but is awake by 4pm.

 **7pm. Quiet play time:**

Start quiet play time sitting him on your knee reading stories and playing with interactive toys such as the Lamaze dragonfly. Turn off bright lights and switch off the TV. Play soothing, relaxing music; have quiet play. Start the bedtime routine when you see the signs of tiredness such as a whiny cry, rubbing eyes and yawning.

 **7.15pm. Last milk feed:**

Give the last milk feed in the lounge, before bath time, to prevent a milk-sleep association and stop feeding if your baby is falling asleep. Babies do not need to drink large quantities of milk to sleep well, it is their ability to self-settle that influences their sleep potential. If you are worried that your baby is not taking enough milk, offer the feed earlier the next night.

### 7.30pm. Sensory playtime:

Take your baby to their room prior to the bath for some sensory play. Your baby's bedroom should be their favourite room in the house, not your bedroom or the lounge. To encourage a positive sleep association with the room, place your baby in the cot and switch on the cot mobile.

Brighten the room with fairy lights and a light show. Play classical music, nature sounds or any relaxing music. Entertain and play with your baby while they lie in the cot. Do not be too concerned if your baby becomes quite excited; he is enjoying quality time with you.

Have nappy-free time while you sing, read, or just chat to your baby; chat about all the different things you did together. Spend quality time for 15 minutes or until your baby starts to cry.

### 7.45pm. Bath time:

Start bath time when your baby shows signs of being bored or tired. Have fun in the bath as your baby is using up his last amount of energy. Dress your baby in the bathroom or their bedroom and avoid taking them into other rooms as it disrupts the flow of the routine.

### 8pm. In the cot:

- After the bath lie your baby down in the cot, dressed in their sleeping bag.
- Turn off all lights except the red glow, position the light so your baby can gaze at it.
- Give your baby their comforter and teddy and let your baby play with any toy until they are ready to snuggle into their sleeping position.
- Remain passive and quiet in the room, occasionally move your baby's teddies and comforters to their face. If your baby cries interact using your voice in an encouraging way: "you're so tired, come on now, sleepy time".
- Until you are confident about leaving your baby, stay in the room until they are asleep.

Use toys with the distraction method if your baby cries

The Lamaze DragonFly (bottom right) is a popular sensory cot toy

- As soon as your baby is asleep turn off the red light and sleep sound. Move the comforter into their hand.

### What to do if your baby resists and cries

All babies sound frustrated and unhappy when they learn new sleep associations. Being awake in the cot is a new experience for some babies. I recommend parents empathise and understand how difficult this is for their baby. Therefore, to make the process as easy for your baby as possible, apply distraction techniques. This requires patience, persistence and gentle perseverance.

Your baby's personality will determine how quick and easy it can be. Some babies have determined characters and resist being distracted. All some parents needed to do is tap the side of the cot, click their fingers, move the Slumber Buddy light about the nursery or gently shake a rattle to get their baby's attention. Once you have stopped the cry, stop the distraction immediately. Reassure your baby with positive praise, and use the baby sign for OK and sleep (place your hands together and at the side of your face). Babies as young as five months recognise this sign and will understand what you want them to do.

Some older babies are not interested in looking at magic shows and need more distraction. Place a VTech toy like 'Alfie Bear', or similar, in the cot and switch it on for a second or two. VTech books that play nursery rhymes or animal noises are also very effective at distracting an older baby. Leave the book in the cot and let your baby play and press the buttons. Choose your baby's favourite toys. Your baby may want to play in the cot for 5-10 minutes before he is tired enough to sleep.

Once babies are truly tired and ready to self-settle, they will start the tired baby cry. Do not distract or intervene. Give them the time and the opportunity to self-settle. Once your baby has learnt how to self-settle, they will need to practise it five-six times before it becomes a habit. Then your baby will settle down to sleep without a peep.

### What to do during the night

Aim to feed your baby approximately six to eight hours after the last feed. Only newborn babies need three to four hourly feeds during the night.

- If your baby wakes and is not due a feed wait until your baby's cry escalates then go in and switch on the sleep sound and sleep light and stroke your baby's head, nose, eyes and mouth with a teddy comforter. Avoid moving your baby as they will expect to be picked up and fed etc.

- Only pick your baby up and take out of the cot to feed.

- Distract your baby from crying by moving the light show and using your voice in an encouraging way: "come on sleepy baby you can do this".

- When your baby wakes up for a feed, feed in the nursery chair and then put your baby back down awake into the cot with the red light, sleep sound and stroke your baby's face with their comforter until asleep.

- As soon as your baby is asleep switch off the red light and sleep sound. Put the comforter in your baby's hand.

### How to de-stress your overtired baby during the day

Babies become overtired when they become over stimulated. The sensory world is all around us constantly, day and night, but most adults know how to switch off, chill out and relax. Babies are constantly bombarded by stimulating environments and do not know how to relax as they have no control of their environment. Overtiredness causes babies to be irritable, cry more, play less, feed more for comfort and use the dummy more. It is therefore quite difficult for babies to self-soothe and they become reliant on mummy to help them relax and de-stress.

### Sensory playtime in the nursery during the day

When your baby appears restless and irritable, this is an indication that your baby is overstimulated and needs a quiet period away from the stimulating environment. The best environment to do this is in the bedroom or nursery, where your baby sleeps. Taking your baby to their bedroom for a chill out session is quality time together and the best form of interaction with your young baby. Create a sensory atmosphere, darken the bedroom, switch on the fairy lights or a morphing light show, play soothing music, nature sounds, classical music or nursery rhythms and sit with your baby on your knee. Read, chat, sing or recite nursery rhymes. Stay in the room until your baby is bored and restless; let your baby lead the session. This is such a positive bonding experience for you both and has long lasting benefits. Two 15-20 minute sessions a day are long enough to de-stress and prevent overtiredness, which so many babies seem to suffer from. Your baby will signal when he has had enough quiet play. Once the session is over, leave the room as it is time for active play.

### Day naps

The Multi-Sensory Sleep Techniques and Routines are perfect for day naps. Babies this age usually like two to three hours of sleep a day; aim for at least one day nap, in their cot, lasting an hour. The timings of day naps vary quite considerably, with some babies having three naps a day while other babies prefer two. Let your baby lead the sleep and indicate when they are ready for a nap and not just bored; one yawn is not a tired sign. When your baby wakes from a nap, give a milk feed. Sleepy milk feeds are ineffective feeds, very addictive and will create a milk-sleep association.

Babies who spend 10-15 minutes a day playing in their cot have a positive attachment to their cot and therefore enjoy being in there. I recommend that mums take their baby to the nursery and have fun time in there every day for stories, chats and playtime, looking up at the mobile. So many babies only go into their cot at sleep times and consequently have a resistance and negative association with the room. A play time in the nursery might lead into sleep time, but not necessarily. Babies only have an attention span of about 15-20 minutes before they are bored and want a change of scene. When your baby has been awake for two to three hours, they are most likely ready for a nap in the cot. Babies can look tired and yawn, but may not be ready for a nap, in which case play in the lounge for a bit longer before starting the routine. Use the same settling process during the day. Babies sleep better in darkness, so close the curtains and put up blackout blinds. Put on the relaxing sleep music and a soft glow light, sit your baby on your knee, facing the lights, for a story, then put your baby down into the cot with their comforter and leave. Switch off the lights and music when your baby is asleep.

# How to solve a sleep problem

Here are three sleep problems in babies aged three to six months.

## Feeding to sleep – breast/bottle

Babies that fall asleep during a feed will develop a milk-sleep association; feeding to sleep feels completely natural but, unfortunately, feeding to sleep is counterproductive. Babies from three months onwards are very aware of any changes, especially if they are in REM sleep cycle. They sense that they have been moved and are not where they fell asleep. Within 40 minutes, babies will wake up and cry for their sleep association i.e. the bottle or the breast. I have known babies to continually wake every two hours throughout the night and expect to be fed again, otherwise they cannot physically settle back off to sleep. I have seen how exhausting this is for mums, as many have not had more than a few hours' sleep at night since the day their baby was born. Breastfeeding mums share identical stories: one mum was woken every hour by her baby who wanted just an ounce of milk to settle him back to sleep. Frequent night feeds impact negatively on the daytime feeds; the baby's appetite is reduced, and they become too tired to feed properly so they snack rather than take a full feed, and the day's structure or routine is disturbed. The easiest way to stop your baby feeding to sleep is to separate milk feeds from sleepy comfort feeds.

- Make a start during the day; aim to feed your baby three-hourly
- Establish a routine when your baby wakes up in the morning and you start the day with a feed, followed by play time, entertaining your baby until he/she is tired and ready for a sleep
- Avoid feeding your baby before a sleep
- If your baby has been awake for a few hours and is nearly due a feed, encourage the nap without a feed
- Take your baby out in the car or pram for their nap and then feed when your baby wakes

- Always give the last milk feed before the bath and not after the bath – a very crucial and important part of reducing a milk-sleep association

Repeat this approach at every naptime until your baby stops expecting to be fed prior to a nap. You will find your baby feeds better after a nap, is more alert and takes more milk. You might take a few days to establish this technique, but, once you have, your baby is ready to progress.

### Rocking and cradling to sleep

'Rock-a-bye babies' like to be cuddled and held firmly. They have a touch-sleep association. Babies are soothed and calmed by a rocking motion; the motion of the car sends most babies off to sleep in minutes; in extreme cases, some babies prefer to sleep in the car seat and nowhere else. Here are two case studies:

### Sophie

Five-month-old Sophie developed a habit of sleeping in the car seat and she would only sleep in her car seat at night. She cried and became hysterical if she was placed in the cot.

'Rock-a-bye babies' like a firm touch to help them relax to sleep, therefore, to replicate the close feeling of the car seat Sophie was placed on her side, in the cot, and her mum, Sarah, gently patted her arm. As soon as Sophie started to relax Sarah gradually stopped patting her and left her to sleep. Sophie's mum gradually stopped patting her arm and left her to self-settle without touch. When Sophie woke up from her nap Sarah fed Sophie and then they went out in the car; this time Sophie stayed awake and did not fall asleep in the car seat.

### Jack

Nine-month-old Jack was rocked to sleep every night as he could not self settle and every time he woke up before midnight his mum had to repeat the same process until he was in deep sleep. Finally after several attempts of rocking him back to sleep Jack would sleep from midnight until 4am before waking again. Jack was nine months old and weighed 21 lbs. His mum was tiny, and she was exhausted; Jack's weight was causing her severe back pain.

- My Multi-Sensory Sleeping Techniques and Routine was introduced
- Tired signs became the signal for bedtime to ensure sleep was baby led
- Jack liked to sleep on his tummy and, because he liked the rocking motion, his mum rocked him gently with two teddies until he was asleep
- When he was relaxed enough and did not cry when placed in his cot, his mum stopped rocking him with teddies and left them for Jack to cuddle

## Waking frequently before midnight

Joshua was three months old when his mum contacted me. She had not been able to get him to sleep for longer than a few hours at a time. He cried more than the other babies in the hospital and his parents were so concerned about him that they had several sessions with a cranial osteopath. Joshua was a breastfed baby and although he had oesophageal reflux his symptoms were controlled with prescribed medication. Joshua was a sensitive baby; during the day he was happy and contented, very inquisitive and noticed everything around him. I observed he was sensitive to any change in his sleeping environment such as sound and touch. This is because during the first few hours of sleep babies are in REM dreaming sleep and are easily woken by any change in their sleeping environment. What babies can see, hear and feel when they drift off to sleep will become sleep associations. When babies are in REM light sleep, they are very sensitive to change and if their sleeping associations have been moved or changed, babies wake up. Joshua needed his sleep associations toning down. His sleep music was reduced in volume and the bright nursery lights switched to a soft red glow. He also slept better when his comforter was placed closer to him so that he could find it more easily. These subtle changes made all the difference to Joshua's sleeping and he stopped waking before midnight.

# Chapter seven

# Co-sleeping breastfed babies

*"Learning how to self-settle is a liberating experience for babies; mums tell me their babies are happier and more content."*

Co-sleeping babies and breastfed babies all have a strong attachment to their mum for sleep, food and comfort. If babies are unable to settle themselves to sleep without being breastfed to sleep they will wake frequently through the night in all the major sleep cycles, four to five times a night. This is exhausting for mum and baby and is unsustainable.

From six months of age babies are naturally more independent and in my experience are happier and more content when they learn to do more for themselves. Learning how to self-settle is a liberating experience for babies; mums tell me their babies are happier and more content.

**In this chapter:**

- Set up the nursery and cot
- How to reduce comfort breastfeeding and breastfeeding to sleep
- Daytime routine
- Bedtime routine

### The benefits of self-settling in the cot are:

When babies learn to self-settle independently they are more relaxed about sleep and enjoy sleeping either in the cot, the car or the pram.

Babies will sleep for longer, reach their full sleep potential and if they do wake in the night it is for a proper feed, not a snack feed or comfort suckling.

The babies appear to suffer less from separation anxiety when mum is out of sight as they are confident about getting themselves off to sleep and don't need mum to help; they can do it themselves.

Mum and baby have quality restful sleep at last.

## Where to begin?

### Set up the nursery and cot

If you are co-sleeping I recommend safe sleeping. To transition your baby to sleeping independently from your bed to a cot, use a Sleepyhead mattress or a similar mattress. The mattress will provide your baby with their own safe sleeping space in your bed and the mattress is easily transferred into your baby's cot.

Introduce your baby to their sensory nursery. Start using the cot for play sessions every day. Make this a fun experience for both of you. If your baby is under six months, attach a battery-operated mobile such as the Fisher Price rainforest mobile or similar projector light show to the cot. Animate the teddies and have a puppet show with them. Play music and nursery rhymes, and let your baby play with their favourite toys in the cot. When your baby is bored and had enough, cot playtime is over. Babies over six months old can sit in the cot with their favourite toys and books. A plastic Tupperware box or shoebox is ideal, fill with colourful clothes pegs, food bag clips and small shakers; babies are naturally inquisitive and will want to sit down and look inside.

 At sleep time, introduce sensory sleep attachments such as a Slumber Buddy or Ewan the Dream Sheep. The red light is soothing to the eye and sleep sounds such as waves or heartbeat are hypnotic. Waves are more soothing for sleep than nursery rhymes. Close the curtains as the sleep hormone melatonin is produced in darkness and your baby will sleep for longer in a darkened room.

Introduce a comforter or teddy and give it to your baby when you are feeding. While your baby is drifting off to sleep, put the teddy's paw in your baby's hand and stroke their face and forehead with it. It is okay if your baby grabs for the teddy and tries to bite it. Only use teddies recommended from birth. The Jellycat range is fabulous.

# How to reduce comfort breast-feeding & breastfeeding to sleep

 Stop all comfort feeding, snacks and feeding to sleep during the day. My sleep techniques will only be effective if your baby has breast milk only at feed times and doesn't fall asleep at the breast.

Breastfeed three hourly during the day. This is so easy to do and the benefits are, your baby will feed eagerly and will be satisfied until the next feed, however babies love to suckle an empty breast. I have observed babies nip the nipple in such a way to prevent the milk flowing. Be aware of comfort sucking – it feels like a flutter and soft flicking sensation. Babies love doing this and it is very addictive.

 Monitor how long it takes for your baby to feed and empty your breast of milk. Check your breasts and feel for lumps. Babies over three months are efficient feeders and hungry babies can empty a breast in five minutes, the feeding action is suck, swallow, gulping the milk down. Babies often come off the breast, pause for breath and start actively feeding again.

## Daytime routine

Follow the 'Day nap routine 3-6 months' on page 103, in Chapter six, What to expect in babies aged three to six months, and implement a day nap routine before you proceed to bedtime.

# Bedtime routine

Follow the bedtime sequence for your baby's age then after bath:

* Sit baby on your knee, reading a book until drowsy and settle your baby as per the daytime routine.

* If your baby wakes up before midnight and is not due a feed, resettle in the same way as before. When you offer a snack feed it encourages more waking, not less, and your baby may wake up before midnight in hopeful expectation of another snack. If you follow this approach it will naturally wean your baby off snack and comfort breastfeeds.

* If your baby wakes up after midnight your baby has slept through the first big sleep cycle, which is great progress. After midnight your baby will be ready for a proper feed. Offer both breasts; hungry babies can empty a breast in five minutes, so encourage your baby to take all the milk but swap to the other breast when your baby starts comfort suckling.

* Put your baby back in the cot, drowsy but awake.

* Stroke your baby's face, mouth and nose with the comforter until asleep.

After repeating this technique for three to four nights you will find your baby is more relaxed about going in the cot and will sleep longer. Now is the perfect time to take your baby to the next level of self-settling.

* Instead of sitting your baby on your knee put your baby straight into the cot after the bath.

* Give your baby some teddies or crinkle toys to hold, i.e. something to look at and something to hold.

* Position the red glow of the Slumber Buddy where your baby can stare at the red light.

* If your baby starts to cry distract him occasionally with a noisy toy and use your voice in an encouraging way. Be

a cheerleader for your baby: *"come on, good boy, you can do this, you're a sleepy boy"*. This approach is hands off the baby, stay in the room, remain calm and passive and wait for your baby to relax into sleep.

 As soon as your baby is asleep remove any toy that makes a noise, leave the teddies, switch off light and sound.

If you can persevere and do this for seven nights your baby will make a positive attachment to the cot and enjoy sleeping.

After seven consistent good nights of self-settling you should be able to put your baby straight into the cot with their teddies and comforter and leave the room. Watch as your baby snuggles down with their comforter and teddies and goes off to sleep without a peep.

The only thing that will interrupt this process is if your baby continues to use the breast for comfort and/or falls asleep at the breast during the day or night. Babies have a strong urge and desire to use the breast for comfort and sleep and this will always be your challenge while you are breastfeeding.

In my experience the mums who restrict breastfeeds to mealtimes only continue to breastfeed successfully after one year when their baby naturally self weans off the breast.

# Chapter eight

# What to expect in babies aged six months to one year

*"To ensure your baby develops natural sleep circadian rhythms, I recommend that all sleep is baby-led."*

Most of my referrals come from parents with a baby aged six months to a year. My theory is that, by the time the baby reaches this age, parents realise their baby is not growing out of bad sleeping habits. In fact, the sleeping problem has got worse and they are now sleep-deprived and desperate for help. Months of sleep deprivation influences all aspects of family life, especially parental relationships; many dads have been sleeping in the spare room for months, while their baby co-sleeps with mum. In addition, babies are making rapid changes in their physical, emotional, social and language development. They are learning to roll over onto their tummies, crawl and pull themselves up to stand. Language develops from a single babble to continuous babble, with the odd word. Their personality is emerging and this is when parents witness personality traits such as frustration, anger and temper tantrums. Many parents are unhappy, and feel they have done something to upset their baby. Frustration, anger, confusion are normal human emotions exacerbated by lack of quality sleep. Your baby will be calmer, more relaxed, less frustrated and happier when they make positive sleep associations. Follow my Multi-Sensory Sleep Techniques and Routines and your baby will reach his age related sleep potential.

**In this chapter:**

- How much sleep does my baby need?
- Multi-sensory sleep techniques
- Bedtime routine
- What to do if your baby stands up in the cot
- Frequently asked questions relating to sleep problems in babies aged six months to one year

### How much sleep does my baby need?

Healthy, full term babies can sleep 12 hours in 24 and the majority of babies are capable of sleeping for 8-10 hours at night without waking. Babies aged six-months to one year are very active and use up lots of energy, therefore they benefit from at least one hour of sleep at lunchtime. Your baby's bedtime will vary slightly depending on their activity during the day; limit the day naps to a total of one to two hours a day as too much sleep during the day will encroach into night sleep. You cannot compare your baby to other babies as some babies need more sleep than others. Every baby has his own unique age related sleep potential and it cannot be increased. To ensure your baby develops natural sleep circadian rhythms, I recommend that all sleep is baby-led, and not coerced mum-led sleep. Be respectful and wait for your baby to be truly tired before settling your baby down for a nap.

### Tired signs

One yawn is not a true sign of tiredness, babies can trick you into thinking they are tired when they are just bored. Try moving to another room and giving your baby another toy to play with. In my experience, mums have difficulty recognising when their baby is tired enough to sleep: a true sign of tiredness is three or four yawns, with eye rubs and whining cry. Starting the routine too soon is counterproductive and escalates into power battles at sleep time.

# Multi-sensory sleep techniques

Never underestimate the effect of sleep associations on your baby's age related sleep potential they can affect your baby's sleep in a negative or positive way. Encourage positive sleep associations by implementing my Multi-Sensory Sleep Techniques.

### Create a multi-sensory nursery

Positive sleep associations start in the nursery, which is an important place as your baby spends 12 hours a day in there. Therefore, the environment should be relaxing and an enjoyable place for you and your baby. First, prepare the nursery: lower the cot mattress before your baby can crawl and pull up himself to a standing position, if your baby had a mobile, detach the mobile from music unit and darken the room with blackout blinds.

### The following are positive sleep associations:

 **Sight**

Sight-sleep associations: fairy lights; star and moon shapes on the ceiling; morphing nightlights; projector light show or a Slumber Buddy that has sparkly lights and plays sea sounds, which can be very hypnotic and soothing.

 **Smell**

Sprinkle aromatherapy oil or scent a comforter with your personal smell.

 **Sound**

Play nursery rhymes, classical music, nature sounds.

 **Touch**

Teddies or a comforter.

Use toys at bath time for a fun sensory experience

A bath seat for six- to twelve-month-old babies

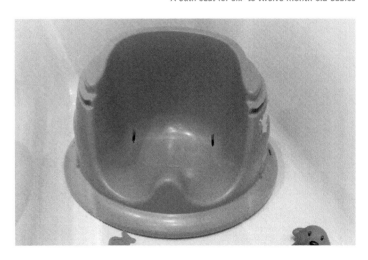

# Daytime routine

If you are new to this approach, I recommend you implement the multi sensory sleep routine with a day nap before proceed to bedtime. Follow the day nap routine in Chapter six.

# Bedtime routine

If your baby is normally asleep by 8pm, this is a sequence to follow.

I recommend you do not let your baby sleep after 4pm and encourage active playtime before 7pm. Aim to start the bedtime routine at approximately 7pm but be guided by your baby. When your baby rubs his eyes, yawns and has a whiny cry, this is the cue to start the bedtime routine.

**7pm. Quiet playtime**

At 7pm turn TV off and dim the lights in the lounge, play relaxing music and incorporate a period of quiet play, stories and cuddles. This signals the start of the bedtime routine.

**7.15pm. Supper**

Give your baby a last feed in the lounge. Milk is an important part of your baby's diet, but to avoid a milk-sleep association, do not give milk after the bath. When your baby is eating three meals a day, offer supper instead of the breast or bottle. Some suggestions are cereal and banana, yogurt, or dairy-free yogurt if your baby is allergic to milk.

**7.30pm. Sensory playtime in the nursery**

Go up to the nursery for sensory playtime, switch on the sensory lights and music. Babies love looking at lights and fairy lights and light shows create an appealing sensory atmosphere. If you have been following this approach from birth, your baby will love this bedtime sequence. Preferably, sit your baby in the cot with his favourite toys or, alternatively, read stories or have cuddles on your knee. This is a good time to incorporate nappy-free time into the routine. The ambience in the nursery is still relaxing and 'womb like with stars'. Relax and enjoy this quality time together, allow your baby to lead the play; they will indicate when they have had enough.

### 7.45pm. Bath time

Now give your baby a bath, this is a fun time and your baby is using up the last ounce of energy. Where possible, dry and dress your baby in the bathroom and avoid walking about with your baby or going into other rooms. If your baby can pull himself up to a standing position, or is crawling, stop using sleeping bags, as they are restricting and your baby could trip and fall. Now go straight back into the nursery; be quick, as the warm, cosy effect of the bath only lasts 20 minutes.

### 8pm. In the cot

Once in the nursery:

- Turn off all bright lights except a focal red glow light
- Switch the sleep music to sea sounds, as they are very hypnotic
- Reduce the volume of the sleep sound
- Sit your baby in the cot
- Give your baby their comforter/teddy and any favourite toy; some babies want to delay sleep time for a few minutes
- Sit on the floor by the cot, but do not lean over the cot, touch or move your baby. Let your baby find his own sleeping position. Parental intervention and interaction is counterproductive
- Distract your baby from crying; say, "*Sleepy time, lie down,*" and give him his teddy to hold; every time your baby cries, repeat "*Sleepy time,*" and pat the mattress with your hand
- Give the thumbs up and the baby sign for sleep (place your hands together and at the side of your face) to reassure your baby everything is okay

Suitable sensory cot toys to use with distraction methods as previously discussed

Interactive books for quiet sensory play time in the cot

135

- If you have a Slumber Buddy, move the red glow light about to distract your baby from crying
- When your baby lies down into a sleeping position, either stay in the room out of sight, or leave the nursery
- Watch on the baby monitor
- Switch off all lights and music when your baby is asleep
- Leave teddies and comforters close by so your baby can reach for them

### What to do if your baby stands up in the cot

Let your baby play and move about the cot, do not be tempted to interact at this stage, i.e. touch or chat to your baby. Let your baby roll, crawl or pull himself up to a standing position, keep neutral and just sit on the floor by the cot and watch, do not lay your baby down or pick him up. Wait until your baby is ready to settle into his preferred sleeping position. Say encouraging words such as "*Sleepy time, lie down,*" and pat the mattress with your hand, this helps babies to understand what you want them to do. Sit on the floor next to the cot and avoid eye contact. Leave your baby to find his preferred sleeping position in the cot; when babies can roll over, some prefer to sleep on their tummies. Babies are naturally independent and if they are physically able to do something on their own, it is common sense and baby-led to let them.

### An alternative to 'cry it out'

All babies cry when they are tired; the only cry you should not be worried about is the 'tired baby cry'. This is a low volume, moaning cry with babies closing their eyes and they rub their faces. Do not interact with your baby or interrupt the sleep 'spell' as your baby is minutes from self-settling and going off to sleep. Do not leave your baby to cry before you pick up, feed or cuddle him it is counterproductive and will cause a negative association with the routine. Instead, distract your baby with a noisy toy, hand your baby their teddy and repeat the key words. Keep this up until your baby starts to settle and relax.

## Hysterical cry

To prevent any hysterical crying, do not start the bedtime sequence too early or your baby will fight sleep and become very angry and frustrated (bear that in mind for the following evening). If your baby is crying hysterically calm them down and lift from the cot, sit your baby on your knee facing outwards towards the red glow light, keep your body language neutral and relaxed and avoid cuddling and rocking but support your baby. When you sense your baby is relaxing and closing his eyes, quickly put your baby back into the cot. Your baby is now minutes from sleep.

## Daytime sensory play

Babies who only go into their cot at sleep times have a resistance and negative association with the room. To increase a positive attachment I recommend you and your baby spend 10-15 minutes every day in the nursery, sit your baby in the cot with toys and books; this is a restful and peaceful time for stories and chats. If the allotted time for sensory playtime is after lunch, it is likely to progress to a nap. Close the curtains to encourage the production of the sleep hormone melatonin, switch on the sleep light, sleep music and give your baby their teddy/comforter. If you have the timing just right, your baby will be asleep in 15-20 minutes. Aim to leave your baby to self-settle and drift off to sleep, go downstairs for a few minutes. If your baby shows no signs of tiredness, go back to the lounge for more active play and try again in an hour's time.

## The overtired baby

Parents describe their baby to me as being over tired and difficult to settle. In my experience the overtired baby is one that has been over stimulated and not had enough restful periods of sleep during the day. Babies rely on their parents to control and change their environment and they can become fractious and irritable if they are overstimulated. It helps if babies can relax and unwind with mummy in the sensory nursery for at least 20 minutes every day. This period of relaxation may not result in sleep, but it is a special bonding experience with your baby.

**Points to consider for day naps**

- Let your baby lead the sleep and indicate readiness for a nap; avoid coercing and forcing your baby to have a nap

- Check your baby is not just bored, as one yawn is not a tired sign, in which case play and entertain baby for longer

- Avoid putting your baby down for a nap too early as they will resist and become very upset; this can lead to a negative association with the cot

- Most babies aged six months to one year like to have one to two hours sleep a day

- Some babies need one nap while others still need three naps a day; on average, if your baby has been awake for four hours, he is ready for a nap

- Aim for at least one day nap in their cot, lasting an hour

- If your baby has day naps in the car or pram, wake your baby after 20 minutes and plan a longer nap after lunchtime in the cot

- If your baby has two hours' sleep during the day, it is logical to assume that they will only sleep for 10 hours at night; hence, it makes perfect sense to reduce the number of hours your baby has during the day, to synchronise your baby's sleep with your own

**Weaning**

From six months, babies are having four meals a day: breakfast at 8am midday lunch, 4pm tea and 7.15pm supper. If you are breastfeeding, feed your baby at mealtimes. This signals to your baby that breast milk is food and not for comfort. Sleepy milk feeds are ineffective feeds and your baby is using the breast for comfort. This is a very addictive habit and creates a milk-sleep association, the main cause of sleep problems in babies aged between six months and one year.

**Dummies**

Dummies are very soothing and comforting for young babies, but as babies get older, the dummy has a negative effect on sleep and is one of the main causes of disturbed nights in babies aged six months to one year. Babies settle well initially, but wake up frequently looking for the dummy.

# Frequently asked questions for babies six months to one year

### Q. I am about to start the Multi-Sensory Sleep Routines. I am nervous about what to expect.

**A.** Parents are naturally nervous the first night. First, create a sensory sleeping environment and spend a few days getting everything together. Lower the cot mattress if your baby is over six months old. If your baby comfort breastfeeds, reduce this before you begin.

### First night

If parents start the routine too early, their baby will cry and become hysterical. I recommend parents start the routine 30-45 minutes later than normal. If the timing is right, babies start the 'tired baby' cry as soon as they are in the cot after the bath. Parents have commented that their baby enjoyed the sensory playtime in the nursery; their baby did not miss the milk feed after the bath and settled more easily than they expected. The parents are relieved and empowered by the new technique.

### How to respond during the night

If your baby has been waking persistently at the same time every night, that pattern of behaviour will continue for a few nights. Resettle your baby the same way as you settled your baby at bedtime. Your baby will adapt quicker to the new routine with positive reinforcement. Hungry babies normally wake between midnight and 4am, so aim to offer milk breast/bottle during that period, not before. You will still be present in the room, reassuring and distracting your baby from the escalating cry, but, normally, your baby will be asleep in half the time and sleep longer before waking up. It is important to be consistent and not change your interventions. Keep up positive reinforcement and resettle in the same way as bedtime.

### Second night

Babies settle much quicker than the first night, but there is still resistance. Babies usually sleep longer before waking.

### Third night

This is when a miracle occurs and your baby settles off to sleep with the minimum of fuss. It is still early days and nights! Consistency and perseverance is the key to success. Your baby has not reached his full sleep potential, which will develop in the next few nights. Quality night sleep affects the day naps; babies do not want a morning nap and are ready for a day nap halfway through their day. Let your baby lead his sleep; he has more energy to stay awake for longer between naps. Avoid coercing your baby to have a nap when they are not ready; one yawn and an eye rub is not a true sign of tiredness.

### Fourth night

Your baby has learnt how to self-settle but you are still part of the settling process; now is the time to retreat. If you have been moving the lights, or touching your baby while they settle, stop doing this and stand back from the cot, sit away out of sight and only respond if your baby sounds distressed. From experience, I have learned that some parents lean over the cot and are too eager to move the lights to distract their baby from crying. Position the light where your baby can see it and sit on the floor with your back away from your baby. Stay in this position until your baby is asleep and repeat this, if needed, during the night. Keep up the momentum and next time, move further away from the cot until you can put your baby in the cot and leave the room. When your baby is asleep, switch off lights and music. This will make a huge improvement to your baby's sleep potential.

### Fifth night

Leave the room before your baby is asleep. Only return if the cries escalate – give the sleep and thumbs up signs, and leave.

### After seven days

After seven days, your baby will be settling off to sleep very well and with the minimum of fuss. However, if you are still part of their settling process and a presence in the nursery, now is the time to back away, leave the room and allow your baby to self-settle.

**Q. My 10-month-old son wakes up for the dummy three to four times a night. How can I stop this?**

**A.** Babies that wake up at night for their dummy have a dummy-sleep association. Dummies are very addictive and babies become very attached to them. To encourage him to put the dummy in himself, stop putting it in his mouth. To lessen the attachment, only use the dummy at sleep times and remove it from his mouth five minutes after sleep. When he wakes up crying for the dummy, go in and put it in his hand, encouraging him to put it in himself. If he throws it away, take the dummy away and leave the room, and wait outside the door. Let him protest for a minute, then go back in and put it in the cot, near enough for him to reach it. When he cries and indicates he wants you to get it for him, pat the mattress and say, "*Sleepy time, here's your dummy.*" Repeat the process until he has gone to sleep. This technique works very well and stops baby losing the dummy for attention. After a week, stop using the dummy for day sleeps and when this has been achieved stop using it at bedtime.

**Q. I am teaching my baby how to self-settle. How do I respond to him when he wakes up during the night?**

**A.** Babies over six months old rarely wake up during the night hungry for milk. If they do wake up, it is for attention and because they need help to resettle themselves back off to sleep. Therefore, I suggest you do not feed your six-month-old baby before 4am. Babies over nine months of age do not need a milk feed before 6am.

If your baby wakes up before the milk feed is due, you respond to your baby in the same way as bedtime but with less intervention. Your plan of action is to go to your baby when the cry is loud and it's evident he's not going to resettle himself. Not at the first peep.

If he is standing up in the cot, do not attempt to lie him down. If he is wobbly and unsteady on his feet, protect him by padding the cot sides with cot bumpers in case he falls. Avoid talking, making eye contact, picking him up or shushing him. If you reach out to touch him, this action could upset him as he will anticipate he is going to be picked up and he will cry even louder. Don't worry if he's standing up, as he will lie down by himself when he is ready. Once you have checked he has only woken up, but is not in pain or suffering from a high temperature, sit on the floor looking at him through the bars, take his comforter out of the cot and hold it. You are going to use it to entice him to lie back down in the cot. Avoid eye contact, switch on the red glow light of the Slumber Buddy and sea sounds.

Say his name firmly and, "*Sleepy time, lie down. Mummy's here,*" and pat the mattress. If he cries in response, repeat it enough times for him to understand what you are saying. He will understand what you want him to do but he will resist as he is not used to you responding in this way. Depending on your baby's personality, the first night can be quite a challenging 'standoff' situation and could go on for an hour, especially if he is particularly stubborn. But if you keep your position, stay calm and speak in a friendly, firm voice, he will lie down and go back off to sleep. He is tired and meant to be asleep. As soon as he lies down, give him his teddy/ comforter and tell him he is such a good boy!

It might take an hour the first time, but patience and perseverance will pay off. If you stay calm, your baby will be less frustrated and confused so by the second and third nights he will not be waking and will be sleeping through the night.

If you are worried about illness and teething causing your baby to wake, I recommend you read Chapter 14, What to expect with babies with health problems.

### Q. My six-month-old has started weaning, but has been waking up at 2am for a milk feed. Is he hungry?

**A.** Babies that have just started to wean often wake up in the night, hungry for a milk feed. The first thing to do is check your baby is having enough milk during the day. Milk is more nutritious than fruit and vegetables, therefore aim to give a milk feed before solid food. For babies who are fussy with food and have small appetites, I recommend they be offered foods with higher calorie content such as banana, puréed sweet corn, avocado, sweet potato, squash, puréed peas, beans and lentils. Without increasing the volume of food, add a teaspoon of butter to vegetables. When your baby is having three meals a day with meat or dairy protein, offer breast/bottle after the food, and your baby will naturally reduce the amount of milk they need.

# Chapter nine

# *What to expect in babies aged one to two years*

*"I recommend classes in baby signing, which are proven to enhance babies' language development and communication skills."*

You have just had a wonderful day celebrating your baby's first birthday with family and new friends! One incredible phase of your life has ended and you are about to embark on another. If you enjoyed the first year of your baby's life, get set for a year filled with lots of fun and laughter; babies aged one to two years are very entertaining, especially when they mirror everything you do. It is fascinating how quickly they learn new words and copy your mannerisms and expressions. Children this age are constantly on the go and can be, at times, particularly challenging. This is the age when you witness frustrations and temper tantrums as your baby learns about rules and boundaries.

**Ten toddler laws:**

1. If I like it, it's mine
2. If it's in my hand, it's mine
3. If I can take it from you, it's mine
4. If I had it a little while ago, it's mine
5. If it's mine, it must never appear to be yours in any way
6. If I'm doing or building something, all the pieces are mine

7  If it looks just like mine, it is mine

8  If I saw it first, it's mine

9  If you are playing with something and you put it down, it automatically becomes mine

10  If it's broken, it's yours

If your baby has a sleep problem, then the year ahead will not be as enjoyable as it might be as lack of sleep can cause stress and tension in parental relationships. Often, parents are too stressed and tired to untangle their baby's complicated sleep problem. My Multi-Sensory approach to sleep simplifies this for parents, the routines guide parents to look at sleep from their baby's perspective, and it gives parents new hope, direction and a plan of action. It is essential that parents have clear knowledge and understanding about their baby's sleep problem, as they are part of the problem and the solution.

### In this chapter:

- Language development
- Separation anxiety
- Multi-sensory sleep techniques
- Bedtime routine
- How to solve sleep problems in babies aged one to two years

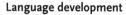

### Language development

Your baby's language will develop, during this period, from a simple babble to three or four word sentences. Some babies are very vocal and articulate. They are real copy cats and repeat everything they hear, but repeating words does not mean they understand the word's meaning. Misinterpretation can lead some parents to have unrealistic expectations about their baby's capabilities. Failure to communicate appropriately can result in everyone being confused and frustrated. Babies understand actions more than words, they are emotionally immature, and have limited rational thought until the age of two to three years; therefore, frustrations and difficulties can express themselves in temper tantrums. In addition, toddlers of this age are also asserting their independence and free will. I recommend classes in baby signing, which are proven to enhance babies' language development and communication skills and reduce tantrums. From a health visiting perspective, 'out of sight, out of mind' works very well too: if children can't see the object they want, they don't remember to ask for it.

**Separation anxiety**

Separation anxiety is a normal phase of child development. Babies enjoy their new physical freedom and independence, but still need, and cling to, their parents for emotional security and happiness. Child psychologists explain the bond between baby and parent is most intense in the age range 12-18 months. Many parents are concerned about their baby's separation anxiety and wonder what to do about it. By 12 months, many mums have returned to work and their baby is with a child-minder during the day. This is when babies experience significant changes in their daily routine. Childcare can influence sleeping patterns, as some babies are at nursery, with the child-minder, grandparents, or a mixture of all three. Therefore, consistency and repetition, with everyone following the same sleep routines, are essential for continuity. Some parents notice that their baby prefers to be with one parent more than the other; from my experience, it is usually mummy, but not always; it is the parent that the baby communicates with emotionally and understands them the most. This can be upsetting for the other parent, but it is a perfectly normal phase of child development and as your child matures, their preferences change.

# Multi-sensory sleep techniques

Never underestimate the effect of sleep associations on your baby's sleep potential; they can affect sleep in a negative or a positive way. Positive sleep associations start in the nursery as this is where babies spend most of their time. Therefore, the environment should be as relaxing as possible and an enjoyable place for you both.

### The following are positive sleep associations:

### Sight

Fairy lights; star and moon shapes on the ceiling; morphing nightlights and projector light shows.

### Smell

Aromatherapy oils or a comforter scented with your smell.

### Sound

Nursery rhymes, classical music and nature sounds.

### Touch

Pillow, duvet, and teddies or comforters. Stop using sleeping bags as they are too restricting and babies can fall over in them. All sleep teddies/comforters should be kept in the bedroom and cot during the day, which acts as an incentive and babies are glad to be reunited with sleep teddy at bedtime. Babies are often too distracted by their sleep teddy and want to hold on to it all day. You will notice that as soon as your baby is interested in a new activity they drop their teddy and walk away from it – if you keep sleep teddy in the cot you will not lose it!

## Bedtime routine

### Tired signs

If you would like your baby to be asleep by 8pm, aim for day nap after lunch and avoid naps after 4pm. I still recommend all sleep is baby-led and not mum-led, therefore wait for the tired signs. These are: rubbing the face, several yawns and an unsteady gait. Babies are less coordinated and fall over when they are tired.

The following is the suggested bedtime sequence for babies who are normally asleep for 8pm.

### 7pm. Quiet play time

Start the bedtime routine with quiet playtime to calm and relax your overtired baby. Dim the lights in the lounge and switch off the television. Put on relaxing a children's DVD and sit together to watch and have cuddles. Wait for the tired signs before starting the next sequence.

### 7.15pm. Supper

Offer your baby a supper of cereal, banana, yogurt, or a dairy-free alternative; if you are breastfeeding, offer the last breastfeed at 4pm. After 12 months of age, to prevent dental decay, dentists recommend all liquids are given in a beaker and to stop using bottles. Milk products are important in your baby's diet, but babies do not need large milk feeds at bedtime, but a snack at bedtime is sufficient to see them through until morning.

### 7.30pm. Sensory playtime

Go up into the nursery for sensory playtime: switch on the fairy lights, light projector or glitter ball (optional!). The ambience in the nursery is still relaxing and 'womb like with stars'. Spend 10-15 minutes on quiet playtime, stories and cuddles. If you have been following this approach from birth, your baby will love this part of the bedtime sequence. Relax and enjoy this quality time together; make it the best part of your day, otherwise babies will sense your tense body language, which will turn into a power struggle and you rush this phase; it might take 10-15 minutes before your baby is ready for a bath. It is more empathetic and respectful if you allow babies to lead the play and they will indicate when they have had enough.

### 7.45pm. Bath time

Now give your baby his bath, brush his teeth and, once dressed, carry him back to the nursery; this prevents your baby running about and getting overexcited. The warm, cosy effect of the bath only lasts 20 minutes, so aim to have your baby in the cot within this time. Babies like to walk about the cot, therefore sleeping bags should not be used; dress your baby in an all-in-one sleep suit.

### 8pm. In the cot

Once in the nursery, dim the lights and reduce the volume of the sleep sound. Sea sounds are very hypnotic. Avoid bright lights and switch on a soft red glow nightlight. Sit or stand your baby in the cot, avoid over handling or lying your baby down, have your baby's favourite toy to hand and let your baby play for a while. Some babies want to delay sleep time and prefer to play with their favourite toy for a few minutes. Watch and wait.

Let your baby play and move about the cot. Do not be tempted to interact at this stage, i.e. touch, or chat to your baby. If your baby is rolling and crawling, pulling himself up to a standing position etc., let him move about; do not lay your baby down or pick him up. Wait until your baby is ready to settle into his own preferred sleeping position. If your baby cries, say encouraging words such as, "*Sleepy time, lie down,*" and pat the mattress with your hand to indicate what you want your baby to do and place their comforter or sleep teddy in the cot. Encourage your baby to find his own sleeping position in the cot; babies are naturally independent so if they are physically able to lay themselves down, it is common sense to let them do so. When your baby settles into a sleeping position, either stay in the room out of sight, or leave the bedroom and watch them on the monitor if you have one. Switch off all lights and sounds as soon as your baby is asleep. Leave toys in the cot, as some babies wake up early and a toy will entertain them for a while.

### Day naps

Most babies aged one to two years still have a nap after lunch, with day naps being phased out by three years of age, some much sooner. I advocate baby-led sleep as every baby has his own unique, age related sleep potential. Most babies sleep for 12 hours in 24 and it is impossible to increase it (see chapter one to read more about sleep potential). Avoid prolonged day naps as they will encroach into night sleep; if your baby has two hours' sleep during the day, it is logical to assume they will only sleep 10 hours at night. If bedtime is 7pm, your baby will be up with the lark and ready to start his day at 5am. If this is too early for you, manipulate your baby's sleep cycle to synchronise with your sleep. If you are back at work, advise your child minder or nursery to wake your baby after an hour. Your baby's activity levels will vary each day and influence how much sleep he requires; aim for at least 10 hours of unbroken sleep at night. This is quality sleep, very energising and beneficial for growth, repair and brain development.

# How to solve sleep problems in babies aged one to two years

The rest of this chapter deals with the most common sleep problems in babies aged one to two years. I have identified their most common sleep problems, which are how to stop:

* Rocking and cradling your baby to sleep
* Your baby making himself sick in the cot
* Your baby waking up at 4am every morning
* Your baby climbing out of the cot

## How to stop rocking and cradling your baby to sleep

*Rock-a-bye baby* is a favourite nursery rhyme and rocking and cradling your newborn baby is one of the joys of being a new parent. However, babies grow up very fast and rocking a 21lb baby to sleep is not a sustainable or pleasurable experience for parent or baby. Some babies aged 12-18 months can weigh as much as 28lbs – in other words, two stones! Many parents are unhappy with how much their baby resists being rocked to sleep and say it feels like a power battle. Babies become angry and distressed if they are rocked to sleep before they are ready. Vigorous rocking and patting your baby to sleep is a form of coercion; it is not baby-led sleep. It is much nicer and more respectful if sleep is baby-led and parents wait for the tired signs before starting any sleep routine.

### Jacob

Jacob was 16 months old when his mum, Ann, contacted me. Jacob's dad was rocking him to sleep as this was the only way Jacob would go to sleep and he was now too big and heavy for her, so her husband did it.

I recommended this routine for Jacob: two days before implementing the changes, Jacobs's mum created a multi-sensory nursery environment for him; Jacob spent 20 minutes every day with his mum in the nursery having quality time together, relaxing, playing, chatting and reading stories.

### First night

After bath time, Jacob was placed in the cot. The key to treating 'rock-a-bye babies' is 'hands off the baby'. This was a new experience for Jacob and I recommended Ann keep her body language neutral but friendly; She made an effort to avoid looking worried or apprehensive, as Jacob was looking at her for reassurance. She kept calm and sat on the floor by the cot, she watched him walk about the cot and throw his toys out of the cot in temper, but she said nothing and stayed calm. Occasionally, Ann patted the mattress and said, "*Sleepy time, Jacob, lie down,*" and placed his sleep teddy where he could reach it. Jacob was very tired and kept yawning and rubbing his eyes. Ann remained very firm but friendly and waited until Jacob sat down and every time he attempted to lie down, she praised him. "*Good boy, Jacob. Yes, sleepy time.*" He stood up a few more times to test Ann's resolve and started the tired baby cry. He was very tired and had very little energy to stand up. It took him a while to get comfortable and decide on the most comfortable position; he rolled about the cot, turning one way then another and it took 30 minutes before he decided to lie down into his sleeping position on his tummy with his bottom in the air. Ann found it hard not to touch him, but agreed it was much easier to put him in the cot and let him choose his own sleeping position. Ann had the option to gently pat his back as he lay down or leave him to self-settle.

At 11pm Jacob woke up and his cry sounded tired but annoyed. Ann went in to reassure him, she did not touch or pick him up, but sat by him and repeated the key works, "*Sleepy time, lie down,*" and after 10 minutes, he settled back off to sleep. He then stayed asleep until 5.30 am, which was their best night ever.

### Second night

Ann repeated the same bedtime routine; Jacob remembered the new routine and settled in 15 minutes. However, when he woke in the night, he was very upset when his dad went into him. If you recall, it was his dad that rocked him to sleep, not his mum, and seeing his dad had reminded Jacob of this so he could not understand why his dad did not pick him up. This highlights the importance of following exactly the same sequence and settling bedtime routine for the first three or four nights, while babies are adjusting to the new routine.

### Third night

Ann decided she would do the bedtime routine and respond to Jacob if he woke in the night. This approach was very successful and Jacob settled in five minutes and did not wake up until 6am. It is normal to expect further progress each night and after a few more days, I recommend parents reduce their intervention (touching, rocking etc.) and leave the room before the baby is asleep.

### After a week

Ann was consistent and persevered with the routine and was amazed at how quickly Jacob adapted to the new routine and could sleep through the night. She noticed he seemed happier, less clingy and whiny during the day, too. Instead of needing a morning nap, he had enough energy to play until lunchtime and had a nap in the afternoon. Babies who suffer from separation anxiety can be helped enormously by being taught how to self-soothe. It is not always possible to be with your baby every waking moment and it is noticeable that babies who self-soothe are generally more relaxed, confident and have less separation anxiety.

### Retreat from the bedroom

Depending on baby's personality, the retreat can be fast or gradual.

I have highlighted a fast retreat as I think it works best. You need to have a sign or signal that you use to indicate you are leaving the bedroom: a few key words will do, something like, "*See you in the morning. Here's teddy.*" Then walk out, close the door and listen, let your baby mess about and play, but if the cry sounds distressed, hysterical or escalates go straight back in; say firmly, but in a friendly way, "*Sleepy time, see you in the morning,*" walk out and keep responding in the same way to the cry until your baby settles to sleep. If it takes longer than 20 minutes, your baby was not tired enough, so delay bedtime by 20-30 minutes. Respond in the same way if your baby wakes during the night.

Never leave a baby crying hysterically; go in at the cusp and nip it in the bud and stay in the room if you have to. Sit away from the cot and ignore it if your baby throws toys out of the cot. Be prepared for tantrums, make no comment turn and walk away. If the tantrum lasts longer than a minute say to your baby, "*Ok, you don't want them? Mummy have them,*" pick the toys up and walk out with them; let the tantrum die down, then say, "Do you want them back?"

### How to stop babies making themselves sick in the cot

It is common for some babies to have such an aversion to their cot that they will gag and vomit as soon as they are placed in it. These babies have an emotional revulsion to the cot and do not see it as a nice place to be; they will scream angrily or hysterically, then cough, which stimulates the gag reflex, until they vomit; this is extreme behaviour and distressing for both baby and parents who can feel guilty. Consequently, parents vow never to let their baby cry ever again! Babies notice that if they behave in a certain way it gets them attention and they make the connection that one way to get their mum's attention is to gag whenever they are put in the cot.

Most parents have been advised at some point by health professionals to leave their baby to 'cry it out' as it appears to be a standard ploy; however, in my experience leaving a baby to 'cry it out' is fraught with complications. I do not advocate or recommend leaving your baby to cry, as it is extremely stressful for baby and parents.

Rafe, at 14 months, had learnt to gag every time he was put in the cot. While he was gagging, he looked at his mum to see what her reaction was. Rafe was communicating to his mum, Suki, in the only way he knew how and basically was saying, "*I don't want to be in here, get me out now and, look, Mummy, I'm going to be sick! You get me out when I am sick!*" This was classic, learned behaviour, and Rafe had been doing it for months.

### This is how we resolved the problem:

Suki implemented my sleep techniques during Rafe's day nap. She waited until he was very tired and did not want to play anymore. She took him up to his cot and stood him in it; instantly, he started to gag, but she stayed calm and friendly, and said quietly, "*Lie down and you can watch Twinkle.*" This worked very well and prevented him from gagging and being sick. She kept up distraction techniques for 20 minutes. The distraction was a nursery rhyme mobile phone app. Suki said he loved them and she used it to keep him amused in restaurants. This worked a treat and he lay down to watch it. The visuals on the phone were so mesmerising, he could not keep his eyes open. After about 20 minutes of repeating the same one and alternating with a few different nursery rhymes a few times, Rafe fell asleep in his cot for the first time ever. Suki followed the same technique at bedtime and, within days, she no longer needed to use the distraction as he was sleeping in his cot without any crying or trying to be sick. This is such an easy, simple way to stop any baby vomiting for attention.

### Babies who wake up at 4am

Waking up around 4am is very common in babies, toddlers and adults as it marks the transition from deep sleep to light dreaming REM sleep. I am often asked about babies who wake at 4-5am every morning, raring to go and ready to start their day and in general, these babies were good at self-settling at bedtime and slept solidly until 4am; however, their mums were convinced their baby was still tired and needed more sleep. I have observed that some babies are genuinely ready to start another exciting day! However, 4am is too early to start your day, so here are a few tips that will help.

### How to stop your baby waking at 4am

Reduce your baby's day nap. Babies aged 12-18 months sleep on average 11-12 hours a day, that includes their day nap. Depending on how active your baby is, I recommend reducing day naps to one hour a day, preferably half way through the day.

Consider the time you start the bedtime routine. It is noticeable that babies who are asleep by 7pm and also have two or three hours of day naps are wide-awake and eager to go at 4-5am. It is important to synchronise your bedtime and sleeping pattern to coincide with your baby. Therefore, I recommend reducing day naps to one hour a day, or delaying bedtime by an hour.

I recommend leaving a few toys in the cot or attaching an interactive cot toy to the side of the cot. It will entertain your baby for a while before they need your attention.

### What to do when your baby climbs out of the cot

Nathan was 16 months old when he climbed out of the cot and his mum, Kerry, found him crying at the top of the stairs. When Kerry contacted me, she was frantic with worry about his safety. Some babies are so agile and active, they can climb out of their cot well before the age of two and the cot is no longer a safe place to be; now is the time to turn the cot into a little bed. Babies who climb out of the cot are at risk of hurting themselves, so the safest option is a mattress on the floor, or a small bed with a bed guard and a safety gate across the bedroom door.

### How we prepared Nathan to sleep in a bed:

Kerry converted Nathan's cot into a bed and used a safety guard to prevent him rolling out during the night. To increase a positive association with his new bed, Nathan's big sister, Claire, sat and played with him every evening after school.

### First night

Kerry followed the Multi-Sensory Sleep Routine and gave Nathan supper instead of a bottle of milk. After his bath, Kerry encouraged Nathan into his bed and as soon as he was under the duvet, she gave him his blanket. Kerry managed to keep him from getting out of bed by sitting close to him and gently moving his legs back under the duvet, and she stayed in the room until he was asleep.

### Second night

Nathan settled at bedtime more easily, but Kerry was still in the room until he was asleep. Nathan was happy to sleep in his bed as long as his mum was with him.

### Sixth night

Kerry started a phased retreat. She said she was leaving, but would be back in a minute; she did this consistently for a week, staying out of his room longer each time until she did not need to return, as he was already asleep. Once Nathan could settle to sleep without Kerry being in the room, he slept through the night.

### Nightmares and night terrors

The youngest baby experiencing nightmares that I met was Angie, 14 months old. Her parents described her behaviour to me: "*She woke in the night before 11pm. She was sitting in her cot screaming hysterically and she did not appear to recognise us and we were unable to console her.*" Naturally, this was very distressing for her parents. I asked more questions to find out what had changed recently.

Previously, Angie had had a sleep problem for a long time, but after implementing my Multi-Sensory Sleep Approach and Routines, Angie had become very good at self-settling and sleeping all night. The major recent change was that Angie had just learned to walk and her mum and dad described her behaviour as 'into everything'.

Any new change in physical development affects babies' sleeping patterns. Active babies and toddlers need extra time at the end of the day to help them to relax, chill and unwind, ready for bedtime.

Angie's parents realised that they had stopped spending quality time before bedtime, as Angie was very good at settling herself. When they reinstated quality chats and story time, Angie stopped having nightmares as she was more relaxed in sleep and made the transition from REM to Non-REM without waking.

This case history highlights that, no matter how good a little one is at self-settling, do not assume they are relaxed. They are probably so exhausted they crash out the minute their heads hit the pillow!

Babies need quality relaxation time just to de-stress and chill before bedtime. Babies and toddlers have the same emotions as adults; they can feel frustrated when they cannot do what they want or have what they want, and easily become overtired and fractious. In addition, their confusion and frustration is compounded by the fact children do not have rational thoughts until they are over two years old.

I recommend parents introduce 10-15 minutes quality relaxation time in the nursery or toddler bedroom prior to the bath and make it part of every bedtime routine.

Even older children benefit from a quiet period before bedtime. This gives your child the opportunity to communicate with you and chat about their day. When you are actively listening i.e. looking at your child eye-to-eye, you are paying your child positive attention. This is the type of attention that produces very positive feelings.

If your body is nice and relaxed in the 20 minutes prior to sleep, this will enhance restful quality sleep; any emotional upset prior to bedtime will influence your REM sleep. You know yourself how hard it is to relax and sleep well if you have had a very stressful day, and how you wake up just as tired as when you went to bed. Babies and toddlers who have disrupted sleep are tired and irritable all day; they, too, need to chill and de-stress at bedtime.

In my experience, some nightmares and night terrors in older toddlers were caused by the children becoming over excited and over stimulated prior to bedtime, so avoid rough and tumble games before bedtime. Most children are unable to relax naturally and have difficulty switching off. You cannot prevent your child having exciting dreams, especially if he has a vivid imagination and is predisposed to them; however, you can control what your toddler watches prior to bedtime.

At bedtime, avoid confrontation and offer a choice of two calming TV programmes, both equally relaxing calming and soporific. Ask your children which DVD they would like to watch, offering, perhaps, *Thomas the Tank Engine,* or a Beatrix Potter tale. Sit and watch it together before going up to their bedroom for quiet games and stories before bath fun time. Encourage your child into bed with the promise of more stories and tell them a tale about when they were little instead of reading more books. Quality time with your baby/toddler makes positive, secure children with happy, long lasting memories. Setting aside 20 minutes of quality time is all the time that is needed to ensure you and your baby/toddler have a good night's sleep.

If you have not found your specific sleep problem, please look in the Frequently asked questions chapter on page 253.

**Quality time with your child**

Special moments make memories that last a lifetime. Spend just 20 minutes of quality time every day with your little one. If you do not have time in the day, bedtime is perfect. To end this chapter, here is a well-known poem which reminds mums to spend time with their child but also look after themselves too.

**Slow Down Mummy**

Slow down, Mummy, there is no need to rush.
Slow down, Mummy, what's all the fuss?
Slow down, Mummy, make yourself a cup of tea,
Slow down, Mummy, come spend some time with me.

Slow down, Mummy, let's pull boots on for a walk,
let's kick piles of leaves and smile and talk.
Slow down, Mummy, you look ever so tired,
come sit and snuggle under the duvet, and rest with me a while.

Slow down, Mummy, those dirty dishes can wait,
Slow down, Mummy, let's have some fun, bake a cake!
Slow down, Mummy, I know you work a lot,
but sometimes, Mummy, it is nice when you just stop.

Sit with us a minute,
and listen to our day,
Spend a cherished moment,
because our childhood won't stay!

**R. Night**

# Chapter ten

# What to expect in toddlers aged two to three years

*"The transition from cot to a bed need not be as daunting as you imagine."*

The toddler years are great fun, but also challenging. Children aged two to three years old start to assert their own independence, learn about rules, boundaries and consequences. For the first time, parents may feel annoyed, angry and frustrated with their child. Most toddlers this age are unable to rationalise, understand adult emotion or use language to articulate how they feel; they will act out how they feel instead. It can be a frustrating and an emotional rollercoaster ride for both parent and child, with lots of tears and tantrums. Do not take your child's temper tantrums personally or be afraid to allow your child to cry; tears are healing they release frustrations, pain and hurt.

Having a good night's sleep makes a huge difference to how parents cope with the challenging demands of their toddler. Here is what one happy family had to say about my sleep routines.

> "Hi Evelyn, I just wanted to say how grateful we are for your help. Amber's sleep has gradually improved over the last month and she has slept from around 7.30 until 6.30 for the last six nights now! I am hoping it will continue. My husband and I are starting to feel human again and I am already finding I am

enjoying the company of both children much more. Thank you for helping us get our life back!" **Helen.**

# Behavioural problems

I became involved in a Positive Parenting programme created by the Family Caring Trust, and for 10 years, I facilitated parenting workshops. The philosophy of positive parenting is child-centred and encourages parents to have respect for themselves and their child.

The following is an extract from the teaching handbook, Pram to Primary (2005). It struck a chord and touched the heartstrings of every parent.

*"Mummy... Daddy... you were so lovely to me in the first year of my life. I knew you loved me and I felt great security, because you looked after all my needs with such attention. I felt precious and secure.*

*What has happened? I miss your smiles and cuddles and all the lovely things you used to say to me. Why don't you notice me much now? Aren't you pleased to see me develop and grow and make my own decisions? Have I done something wrong? Am I bad? Don't you love me anymore? When I couldn't talk you used to listen with big round eyes. When I couldn't walk you paid me such good attention and encouraged every little step. Now you don't seem very interested. I know I misbehave a lot now, but it seems to be the only* way I get your attention these days; I don't like it when you scold me and when you're impatient with me, but I'd rather have that attention than nothing.

Things would be different if you gave me attention when I'm good. I am happy to play on my own and talk to myself and sing, I need you to notice me sometimes when I am good. Please, Mummy, please, Daddy, I miss you. I do love you to pay attention to me when I am not misbehaving. I will misbehave much less if you do.

I need the positive attention you used to give me – the affection and the cuddling and the delight when you looked at me. I need to know you love me and that I am still lovable. Am I?"

*Pram to Primary*, Family Caring Trust

**Four emotions that parents feel when their child misbehaves:**

- **If you feel annoyed:** your annoyance could be a sign that your child is seeking attention.
- **If you feel angry:** your anger is a sign you and your child are in a power struggle.
- **If you feel hurt:** your hurt feelings are often a clue that child is seeking revenge.
- **If you feel helpless:** your helpless feeling is often a clue that your child is showing inadequacy.

When your toddler misbehaves, which they all do, any pre-existing unresolved sleep problem will increase family tension. When parents decide to deal with their child's sleeping problem, they are looking after themselves too.

The following is an example of a frequently asked question.

**My two-year-old whines at me all day to the point where I am in tears**

When you feel annoyed, your child is exhibiting attention-seeking behaviour; this is a vicious circle and the more annoyed you become, the more attention-seeking your child will become. He senses something is wrong, but he does not know what to do about it, and is looking for reassurance and comfort. Children will also whine for their sleep teddy, dummy or blanket. Language development is minimal in most two- to three-year-olds; tantrums and frustrations are exacerbated by the child's inability to communicate effectively.

**Parents can help their child by:**

**Listening**

Listening means giving eye contact and looking at your child when they talk to you. If you repeat a few of your child's words, they will know you were paying attention and understood them and that encourages children to say more.

**Reflecting feelings**

You can empathise with your little one's feelings if you say, *"You look sad," "You look happy," "You look pleased about that,"* or *"You were angry I won't let you do that..."* It will help them to become aware of their feelings.

**Using an 'I' message**

Let your child know you have feelings too by giving an 'I message'. For example:

*"I'm happy you got into bed all by yourself."*

*"I'm pleased you've eaten some carrots."*

*"I enjoyed playing with you today."*

*"I am sorry I was cross with you – I was very tired."*

*"I love you."*

**Notice your child at play**

A simple and easy way to reduce attention-seeking behaviour is to notice your child when they are playing. Give your child attention when he is playing nicely and least expects it. Avoid giving instructions and asking questions. Make noticing statements such as, *"Oh, you're using the red bricks to build your tower."* Refrain from telling your child what to do or how to play with their toys. When you make a noticing comment, your child will happily play for longer; parents find it odd at first, but children really love this attention.

Ignore minor misbehaviour. Instead, give lots of positive praise for good behaviour. Avoid over-exaggerated praise that can sound insincere, like: "*You are marvellous!*" Instead, notice the effort involved: "*Well done. That was difficult, and you tried really hard.*"

# Problems at meal times

Feeding problems are very common in this age group. Most healthy toddlers can be fussy with food; they have small appetites and prefer to snack. Most toddlers are naturally slim, too busy and too preoccupied to eat; they lose interest in eating after 15-20 minutes and if they continually snack on fruit, raisins, biscuits or milk, they will not eat at regular meal times. Consequently, food refusal causes parents to worry and they become over attentive at meal times. If children are reprimanded for not eating, they may react and throw their food or cup on the floor. Constant battles at mealtime will create a negative emotional association with food; this becomes a vicious circle and increases parental concern. To break the cycle of food refusal requires parents to take a different approach.

### Try a new approach

If your child constantly gets down from the meal table before they have finished eating, ask, "*Have you finished your meal?*" Keep your tone of voice and body language neutral and calm. If your toddler indicates "*Yes,*" then clear away their meal and do not allow your toddler back to the table. If your child says, "*No,*" respond with a firm but friendly, "*Come back and when you have finished your meal, you can play.*"

### Follow through with what you say

If you want your child to eat with you at regular mealtimes, do not offer any other food, snack or milk except water until the next mealtime; this can be hard for parents who worry about their child not eating. If you allow your toddler to fill up with milk and snacks between meals, it will reduce their appetite and they will persistently refuse to eat normal meals. Your toddler might protest, demand a snack, and even have a tantrum, but stay calm and neutral; this is the only way to stop this type of behaviour recurring.

### Food battles

To avoid food battles, turn and walk away from the tantrum. Tantrums last longer if they have an audience. Say, "*Okay, I'll put your lunch in the fridge until teatime. Play with your toys while Daddy and I finish eating.*" This will indicate to your child that their mealtime is over. This approach teaches children to eat at the meal table and that getting down from the table before they have finished is not an option. Allowing children to make choices and live with the consequences is respectful and an effective method of discipline. Ultimately, this approach reduces behavioural problems at mealtimes and increases a positive emotion, which increases your child's confidence to be more adventurous with food.

### Portion size

Toddlers have small stomachs, about the size of their fist; therefore, avoid facing your child with too much food on their plate. Most children will naturally control their appetite and eat until they feel full. If your child has become fussy and attention-seeking at mealtimes, give him an empty plate and invite him to help himself from a communal plate. I know children like eating food from mum's plate! Table manners can come later! If you are a 'grazer' then your toddler could have this tendency too, in which case, offer small portions of nutritious snacks and meals. To foster confidence and trust at mealtimes, take this approach when you introduce new foods: "*Have a taste. You don't have to eat it if you don't like it,*" and never force your child to eat. Say something along the lines of, "*After one more spoonful of beans you can have your yogurt.*"

## Power battles

If your child's behaviour makes you feel angry, you are in a power battle with your child. Children hate being told off and if you use a bossy, authoritative tone in your voice, your child will either mimic you or get upset; this will escalate into a power battle. Responsible parents are keen to teach their children about right and wrong, but if your child hears the word *No* too many times a day, he'll become very frustrated and angry; just like adults, children dislike being told what to do. Often, the mornings can start badly simply trying to get your toddler dressed for nursery or play group. Power battles getting dressed can be exhausting, chasing your toddler around the house and cajoling them to get dressed. Instead, tell them about all the lovely things they are going to do when they are dressed. Often just changing the sequence of the morning routine can make a huge difference; for example, if your toddler enjoys watching children's TV, don't put the TV on until he is dressed. Children do understand this type of reasoning, but remember to follow through with what you say; children's behaviour dramatically improves with consistency and repetition.

### Give your child a choice

If you have battles over clothes, it is respectful to give your toddler a choice: you choose two T-shirts and let them decide which one they would like to wear or ask your toddler, *"Do you want to dress yourself or shall Mummy dress you?"* This approach works well in every situation where conflict and power battles arise. Life is so much calmer when you give your child a choice, which increases their confidence and independence, especially when they start playgroup and you are not there to help them.

### Avoid the *No* word

I recommend to all parents to avoid being confrontational and stop using the *No* word for misbehaviour; it is counterproductive and attracts more attention to the behaviour you want to avoid. It is more respectful to distract your child's attention away from the object, for example, if your child plays with daddy's keys, say something like, *"They're Daddy's keys. Put them here so Daddy can find them. Now, where are your toys?"* This approach works for any situation, which involves your child taking possession of an object you do not want them to have. If your child refuses to tidy away the toys, make a game of who can put them away the quickest: use the words as soon as before you give an instruction. *"As soon as we have tidied the toys away, we can watch TV."* It is such a simple, easy thing to say, it is very respectful, and your toddler will happily comply.

### Distraction and role-play

Two- to three-year-olds like to be helpful and be involved with any activity with you, e.g. cooking, baking. Within reason, allow your child to help. If you are doing something that is inappropriate, negotiate with your toddler to do something else while you are busy. Choose an activity that will keep them absorbed and interested; however, be realistic: children have short attention spans and are only capable of watching TV for 15-20 minutes.

## Moving from cot to bed

### At what age do you move your toddler to a bed?

Many parents fear their wonderful sleep routine will unravel when their toddler goes into a bed. Making the transition from the cot to bed depends on your toddler's physical size and contentment in the cot. Most toddlers I know are contented and sleep well in their cot up until the age of two or three years, while others climb out as soon as they are physically able to do so.

### If your toddler climbs out of the cot

When your toddler can climb out of the cot, it is a safety concern and your toddler will be much safer in a little bed. If you are worried about your toddler getting out of bed in the middle of the night, fit a safety gate across your toddler's door. The transition from cot to a bed need not be as daunting as you imagine.

**Positive change**

Think of the positives; moving from the nursery to a larger bedroom is a new beginning. Effectively you are putting behind you all the previous problems around bedtime. More than likely, any earlier fuss and upsetting behaviour would have caused your toddler to have a negative sleep association with the cot. A new bedroom gives you the chance of a fresh start, in a new environment. With new beginnings, you have a new routine and are leaving behind bad memories and bad habits. **Here is how you do it.**

# *Multi-sensory sleep techniques for toddlers*

**Create positive sleep associations with the bedroom:**

* The smell and touch of a familiar sleep teddy or comforter
* The sound of your voice reading the story
* The sight of a night light at bedtime all become positive sleep associations

**Avoid:**

* Starting the bedtime routine too early
* Rushing through the routine, or being impatient
* Using cross words, which is counterproductive and will cause your toddler to misbehave

**Using my techniques, your toddler will:**

* Become an independent sleeper
* Enjoy going to bed
* Snuggle down in his bed with a story and a cuddly toy

**Create a sensory bedroom**

Spend a few days preparing your toddler's bedroom. To create a relaxing and calming bedtime environment, make the bedroom cosy and welcoming. Try:

- Putting colourful pictures on the walls
- Putting up shelves for books and providing boxes for toys
- Keeping the bedroom as tidy and uncluttered as possible
- Darkening the room with blackout blinds; there is an increased production of the sleep hormone melatonin in darkness and your toddler will sleep longer, especially during the summer months
- Using interesting night-lights, fairy lights and Slumber Buddies, remembering that if you choose well, you and your toddler will enjoy them
- Converting the cot bed into a toddler bed, and perhaps providing new bed linen decorated with Disney characters or anything which appeals to your toddler's personality and interest
- Keeping your toddler's comforter, sleep teddy or dummy for bedtime only, leaving them in the bedroom during the day

**Ditch the dummy**

Sucking a dummy can become a very addictive habit and difficult to break; some toddlers like to walk around and talk with the dummy in their mouth all day. Speech therapists and dentists advise parents to restrict the use of the dummy, as it can affect toddlers' speech and cause malformation of the front teeth. One good way of reducing dependency on a dummy is to only use it at sleep times, and once your toddler is asleep, remove it after 20 minutes.

**How to stop giving milk in a bottle**

Drinking milk from a bottle is another addictive habit to reduce and stop. Not only is the sucking action of drinking from a bottle a very addictive habit, it also causes tooth decay due to the sugar content in milk; for this reason, dentists recommend that parents stop giving any liquid in a bottle from 12 months of age. This includes sip/seal beakers.

It is easy to stop offering milk in a bottle. Say to your toddler in a friendly, but matter of fact, voice, *"Bottles all gone, only babies have bottles. You're too big! Mummy can't find them."* Your toddler is going to be very disappointed about this and will need evidence once you have disposed of all bottles and teats; open cupboard doors to prove to your toddler they have gone. Do not worry if your toddler refuses to drink milk from a sippy cup. The recommended amount of milk your toddler needs can be found in yogurts, milk served with cereal, and in cheese. A small pot of yogurt contains 120 ml of milk and there are 250 ml of milk in 30 grams of cheese. A typical toddler diet consists mainly of cheese, yogurts and cereal and they will be getting enough milk protein and calcium for healthy bones.

**Day nap**

Most toddlers aged two to three years sleep 12 hours a day including day naps. Many do not have a day nap and if they do, it is usually for an hour after lunch. Long day naps will reduce the time they sleep during the night and toddlers who have day naps tend to wake very early in the morning; some are up at 5.30am every morning. If your toddler sleeps for an hour after lunchtime and is in bed, asleep, at 7pm, he will wake up and be full of beans and ready to start the day at around 5-6am. If your child goes to nursery, speak to the staff about it. It is unrealistic to expect toddlers to sleep 12 hours at night if they sleep for up to two hours at nursery.

If you would like your child to sleep 7pm until 7am, then stop the day nap. Twelve hours of quality sleep should be energising enough for most toddlers.

**No sleep after 4pm**

Preventing your toddler napping after 4pm is tricky, especially if you are balancing and juggling your day with a toddler and schoolchildren. It is inevitable that an exhausted toddler will fall asleep whilst in the car or pram on the school run. A nap around 4pm could delay bedtime for up to an hour, so, on these occasions,

Entice your toddler into bed to look at the sparkle lights of the Slumber Buddy

be as flexible as possible. If you want your toddler in bed for 8pm, gently wake him after 15 minutes; he will be drowsy, so sit quietly together for a while before joining in with the rest of the family. Then engage your toddler in active playtime.

### Active playtime

Use up surplus energy by playing out in the fresh air, perhaps in the garden or at the park. Allow your toddler to walk as much as they want to and use old-fashioned reins to keep them safe near busy roads. During the dark winter months, turn your lounge into a mini-gym just for an hour!

# Bedtime routine

Many parents have a set time for bed and start a routine at the same time every evening; this can work well if you have a very structured and ordered day routine. If not, it is better to have an extra 30 minutes in the lounge playing nicely, than 30 minutes messing about in the bedroom. Avoid being dogmatic about a set bedtime; your toddler's daily activities will influence what time you start the routine. I recommend that sleep is child-led; wait for your toddler's tired signs of yawning and rubbing their eyes. Some children also start to misbehave and whine.

**This is the sequence to follow for children who are asleep by 8pm:**

**7pm. Quiet playtime**

You and your toddler will be physically and emotionally exhausted at the end of a busy day. To prevent what some parents call 'meltdown', prepare your toddler for bedtime at least one hour before they are normally asleep. A calm and relaxed prelude to sleep will reduce tantrums at bedtime, nightmares and night terrors. Some very imaginative children are predisposed to them and a calm, peaceful bedtime reduces the incidence. The hour before bedtime should be as relaxed and calm as possible. Spend 15 minutes playing quietly together: this is a good time to watch children's TV, read interactive stories or sit and do simple puzzles together; let your child lead the play and decide what they want to do. Avoid any bossiness, conflict and power battles. This can be quite a challenge at the end of the day when everyone is exhausted, but worth it. Your little one will be in bed in an hour!

**7.15pm. Supper**

Most toddlers have tea around 4-5pm, unless your toddler goes to nursery, in which case they have a sandwich, yogurt and fruit around 3.30pm. By 6.30pm, your toddler will be hungry and ready for a light supper: offer a choice of foods that aid sleep such as cereal, toast, banana and yogurt and a drink of water in a beaker. To prevent a milk-sleep association, avoid offering milk. In addition, too much liquid will compromise the possibility of having a dry nappy in the morning. Do not encourage your toddler to drink during the night or leave a beaker in the bedroom.

### 7.30pm. Sensory play in the bedroom

When your toddler is ready, go into their bedroom; let your toddler switch on the night light and choose the stories, place the book on the bed with the sleep teddy/comforter ready for when you return. Be strict about the dummy/comforter; it should remain in the bedroom all day until after the bath. Spend 5-10 minutes in the bedroom preparing the room.

### 7.45pm. Now for some fun bath time!

Bath time can be the best part of a toddler's day, so make it lots of fun. It signals to your toddler that it is bedtime and the bath will become an integral and important part of the sleep routine. Your toddlers may look over active and excitable, but by the time they come out of the bath they have used up their last surge of energy. During the bath, be prepared for water splashes! If your toddler hates having his hair washed, rinse using a sponge or encourage him to lie down in a shallow bath, just at ear level and rinse his hair.

### Brush teeth

Bath time is a good opportunity to brush your toddler's teeth. The molars need particular attention, as children keep them until they are teenagers. Dentists recommend you use a pea size amount of adult toothpaste on a dry toothbrush: adult toothpaste is best as it has the correct amount of fluoride to prevent dental caries.

If possible, dry and dress your toddler in the bathroom and carry your toddler to the bedroom. Prevent your toddler from running around the bedroom or jumping on the bed as this will energise and cause overexcitement, and the warm, cosy effect of the bath will be lost.

### 8pm. In the bedroom

Let your toddler climb into bed himself. Avoid any coercion or impatience, as your toddler will notice your tense body language and misbehave. Entice your toddler into bed with a promise of story time and teddy/comforter; start the story as soon as your toddler is lying down under the duvet; children love hearing stories about themselves when they were little and you may need to read the same story again. Sit at arm's length away from the bed; your toddler had lots of cuddles and kisses earlier and will have more tomorrow. Now is the time your toddler learns how to self-settle and become an independent sleeper; avoid holding hands, patting or stroking. When your toddler snuggles down into their usual sleeping position, lower your voice, then it is your voice that is soothing, not the story.

### What to do if your toddler gets out of bed

When the story has ended, your toddler may think this is the cue to get out of bed; this is when the challenging part begins. The key to the next approach is to keep friendly but firm: your voice needs to be calm and neutral otherwise our toddler will sense your impatience and play up; calmly say, "*Sleep time, back into bed. Here's teddy. Lie down and Mummy will sit here until you are asleep.*" Point to the floor or chair where you are going to sit, do not be tempted to sit on the bed as this is giving your toddler a mixed message. Your toddler may test your resolve; be firm and friendly as your actions speak louder than words. Be prepared to walk out the room unless your toddler gets back into bed, wait outside the door for a minute to prove you mean what you say and then go back in and repeat, "*Sleep time, lie down and Mummy will sit here until you are asleep.*"

Avoid being drawn into a conversation with your toddler; it will be delaying tactics and attention-seeking behaviour. Repeat this until your toddler is asleep, and then turn off the lights and leave the room. In the morning, use an 'I' message: "*I am very happy you stayed in your bed all night.*" This might seem obvious, but young children are confused by adult behavior, so never assume your child understands you. Speech and language studies report toddlers only listen and absorb a few key words in a sentence. Therefore, use short and clear sentences, for example: *Lie down; Sleep time; Here's your dummy/comforter; Mummy read story.*

# How to solve problems at bedtime

Set up the toddler bedroom to be sensory and appealing. If you are worried about your child getting out of the bedroom use a safety gate by the door.

1  Don't start the routine too soon otherwise you will be upstairs for hours wasting time and getting frustrated. The time from bath to bed and sleep is 30 minutes max. Have lots of cuddles and stories in the lounge before bath, not after. Interactive books in the bedroom are too energising and not relaxing enough.

2  I recommend a Slumber Buddy – Bella the Butterfly is lovely for a little girl, and Eddie the Elephant for a boy. They only stay in the bed and toddlers only get to play with them in bed. That is the Slumber Buddy rule; the same applies for a dummy, sleep comforter or teddy.

3  After bath, go straight into the bedroom, don't allow running about as that will energise your toddler. Encourage your toddler into bed, don't lift him in. The previous page has the most relevant information for you.

4  Once he is in bed sit at the side, leaning forward but not touching. If he reaches out for you put a teddy in

his hand and fold your arms. Start to chat about your day together, if your toddler talks and tries to distract you, ignore him but say: *"shall I tell you about tomorrow? Lie down and Mummy will tell you a story"*. Keep chatting until he has lost interest and starts to yawn. Now switch off all lights but he can keep the Slumber Buddy light and play with the buttons. Sit by his side, say *"night"*, give a brief kiss, then no more touching and ignore his conversation, occasionally say *"sleep time"* and wait until he is asleep.

5 Don't leave the room until your toddler is asleep. If he tries to get out of bed, say: *"I'm still here and waiting for you to get into bed"*. Say nothing else; he will soon get bored and climb back into bed. Let your toddler do everything themselves, otherwise he has hooked you in again. Keep patient and wait and wait, there is no rush and tired children are asleep in 10 to 15 minutes.

## What to do in the night

When he wakes at night, leave him for a few minutes, avoid rushing in at the first sound of movement. Go in, say *"back to bed"*, let him climb in himself and then sit on the floor with your back to him and wait until he has gone back to sleep. He can play with the Slumber Buddy until he is ready to settle down.

This is tiring and requires patience but is such a good investment of your time and reaps dividends – a full night's sleep!

When your toddler has made significant progress at settling and sleeping until the morning, now start to do gradual retreat. Give your child a personal belonging of yours, your hair clip or a scarf, and say to him: *"hold this for mummy, I need to go to the toilet and I'll come back and get it"*.

Do exactly that, otherwise your child will be very hurt if you trick them and do not return. This is the best way to build up your child's trust and confidence about being on their own. Once that works, increase the time you stay out of the room until your child is confident and happy to sleep without your presence. This may take a week or two but it is well worth investing your time in as your child will have the confidence to sleep peacefully all night.

## How long does it take the techniques to work?

If you follow the routine and sequence for three to four days, you will see huge improvement in your child's ability to self-settle and sleep all night.

### First night

It can take an hour for your toddler to settle to sleep; the length of time is dependent on how tired, how determined and how stubborn your toddler is. Keep calm, confident and friendly as your toddler will be watching your every move – this is a new experience for them too! They might resort to a few familiar attention-seeking tactics to get your attention, in the hope you will change your mind. There could be frustration, temper and a few tears, but with gentle perseverance and patience, your toddler will resign and go to sleep.

### Waking in the night

When your toddler wakes up during the night, they will have remembered what happened at bedtime and test it out. The approach is the same as at bedtime: go in and say, "*Still night time. Lie down and Mummy will sit here until you are asleep.*" It is time well invested as consistency and perseverance is the key to this approach. Once they have done it the first night, it becomes second nature to them. Gro clocks are very useful.

### Nights three to four

As soon as your toddler is sleeping through the night and enjoys the new routine, start to make a gradual retreat from the bedroom. After the story, give a last kiss and cuddle, and say, "*I'm just outside your door. Snuggle down, sleep time. See you in the morning.*" Listen for any movement and as soon as you hear your toddler getting out of bed, immediately go back in and guide him back into bed; repeat this until he is asleep. The gradual withdrawal from the room could take longer for your toddler, so go at your child's pace and confidence level.

### After a week

Within a week of being consistent and persevering with the routines, your toddler will:

- Be an independent sleeper
- Have made a positive sleep attachment to his bed
- Stop waking in the night
- Stop waking and asking for milk
- Stop needing you to stay in the room
- Be more energised and happier during the day

# Toilet training

**When is the best time to start toilet training?**

By two years of age, most children indicate they have a dirty nappy by patting their nappy and saying, "*Poo.*" They understand when mum says, "*You've done a poo. Mummy change your nappy.*" At this stage, your child thinks it is normal to poo/wee in the nappy and mummy changes the nappy. Now is the time to have a new conversation with your child such as, "*Wees and poos can go in the potty.*" Make it a fact and not a request, as it might be too early for your child to be developmentally capable of using the potty successfully. If your child has not indicated they are ready, wait a few more weeks, but on average, the best time to start toilet training is at age two-and-a-half. Some children, although ready to use the potty, prefer to use the nappy to wee/poo. I once knew a three-year-old boy who preferred to play with his cars in the lounge while he dirtied his nappy. This was not really appropriate for his age and when his mum saw him starting to strain she took him to the bathroom where he finished having a poo and his nappy could be changed. Being proactive prepares your child for the next phase, sitting on the potty.

If your child is ready, most children are toilet trained within a week. Here is a plan of action:

- Have fun choosing new pants together and have several to hand in case of accidents
- Older children like rewards and a sticker chart is a great incentive during the first week; it is an immediate and

visual reminder of their achievement

- Your child will have fewer accidents and be toilet trained quicker if you plan to be close to home for a few days as repetition and continuity speed up the process

- Stop using a nappy or pull-up during the day, even when you go out, as pull-ups are counterproductive to toilet training; when your child is wearing a pull-up, the sensation on their skin is the same as a nappy

- If your child is not dry at night, they may need a nappy for a day nap; children wee in REM sleep

- Take your child to the potty after a drink or after meals. Say, "*Let's see if a wee wee comes?*" Only sit your child for a minute or longer if they are happy to do so. If nothing happens, say, "*Try again later.*"

- Little boys need to learn to wee and poo on the potty, otherwise they will continue using the nappy for a poo; when little boys are fully toilet trained, they can stand up to pass urine, it is very common for little boys to be dry during the day and night, but soil their pants or bedtime nappy

- By the end of the first week, your child will tell you when they need the potty and prefer you to wait outside the bathroom. They will shout "*Ready!*" when they want you to help with wiping and pulling up pants

By the age of two years and six months, the muscle that controls the release of urine has matured and children are able to recognise the urge to wee and they can hold on until they have reached the potty. Some children have accidents and get to the potty a little too late – be very sensitive to little accidents as children are very upset if they think they have done something wrong; say, "*Never mind, next time in the potty.*" Being critical or impatient can lead to behavioural issues with using the potty; conversely, avoid drawing too much attention and using over exaggerated praise when your child does a wee in the potty. A cuddle and pat, with, "*Well done, clever boy/ girl,*" is enough praise. Avoid involving other family members in front of your child as too much attention is very intimidating and makes children self-conscious. Some children like all the praise and attention and try to use the potty again and fail; this confuses and disappoints children. Normalise going to the potty and let your child see you use the toilet and the actions involved – wiping, flushing the toilet and washing hands.

**Where to keep the potty:**

Children of two years are quite accepting of using the potty in the lounge even in front of other people, while older children become self-conscious and embarrassed, in which case, keep the potty in the bathroom.

Once your child is confident using the potty, keep up the momentum and progress to a toilet seat and step.

**Dry at night:**

During Non-REM sleep (midnight until 4am), a hormone is produced to condense urine, which aids dry nights. This hormone is not present in every child under school age. Enuresis is a hereditary condition. However, if you know of a close family member who had enuresis, be reassured; there is help available from specialist school nurses. Most children are dry at night before they are five years old.

You will know if your child has produced the hormone and condensed the urine. The nappy will feel light and dry in the morning. You can tell if your child has just had a wee in the nappy, as it will be very warm and very wet. If you think your child is ready to stop using nappies at bedtime, use a mattress protector in case of accidents. Discourage your child from drinking more than a few ounces of juice/water/milk at bedtime or during the night as it will compromise the chance of dry nights.

**Regression**

Sometimes the novelty of using the potty wears off, especially in little boys. Some are too busy playing and leave it to the last minute and have accidents. Others have a lazy streak in their nature and are not bothered about where or when they have a wee/poo. Often, they just need reminding about what is expected of them and more positive praise. A sticker or star chart will help to keep their focus and interest. Toilet regression also occurs when there has been any major change in their life, such as a new baby in the family, moving house, or starting playgroup or nursery, all of which are a normal part of life and, therefore, after a period of adjustment, the problem resolves itself.

# Frequently asked questions for toddlers

**Q. My two-year-old has just started to sleep in a single bed, but she keeps crying and getting out of bed when I leave the room. I am up and downstairs for several hours until we are both exhausted and she eventually falls asleep. How can I stop this?**

**A.** Your toddler has separation anxiety. Encourage her to stay in her own bed by making the bedroom feel special and a nice place to be; have play times in there during the day, make the room multi-sensory and the best room in the house. Follow the Multi-Sensory Sleep Routine for toddlers.

Encourage your toddler to stay in bed with positive praise and immediate reward. Most two-year-olds can be irrational and unreasonable, therefore actions speak louder than words. You need bargaining tools like a sleep teddy or comforter, and stories. Some children respond very positively to a sleep toy such as a Slumber Buddy. The bedtime rule is that stories and sleep teddy stay in the bedroom and are only given when your toddler gets into bed. Say something like, "*As soon as you get into bed you can have teddy and a story.*" Reward your toddler for getting into bed, with immediate praise and giving the comforter or favourite teddy or reading a story. After the story, give one last kiss and cuddle, keep the night light on and leave the room. Wait outside the door, listening for movement. As soon as you hear your toddler getting out of bed, calmly walk back in, pick up teddy/comforter and say, "*As soon as you get into bed you can have teddy.*" Always follow through with what you say. Your toddler might test this a couple more times, but repeat this until she has gone to sleep. Stay friendly and calm at all times, follow the settling routine and your little one will be asleep in no time! In the morning, praise your child with a cuddle and hug. A star chart also reinforces good behaviour. Avoid rewarding with sweet treats or promising to buy a toy. The reward needs to be immediate and appropriate.

**Q. My three-year-old cries if I do not lie down with him at bedtime and stay until he is asleep. He wakes up in the night and I end up getting back into his bed and falling asleep. In the morning, he is still tired and has tantrums during the day; I am exhausted too. What else can I do?**

**A.** It sounds like your child has become over dependent for attention at sleep time and you are his comfort blanket. He does not need this type of attention at sleep time; he can become an independent sleeper. He will be less whiny and clingy during the day; you and your son will feel better if he can learn to sleep without you. Most three-years-olds have good vocabulary and understanding, so discuss the changes with him. Be positive and upbeat about this; introduce a reward that will encourage his co-operation. Make his bedroom multi-sensory and the best room in the house. Follow the Multi-Sensory Sleep Routine. In three to four days, your toddler will feel confident, secure and happy enough to let you leave the room before he is asleep. Give lots of praise and reward him with a 'Good boy' sticker in the morning.

# Chapter eleven

# Sleep and breastfed babies

*"Breastfeeding has many positive benefits for both mum and baby and is the natural, perfect food for babies."*

My passion and interest in helping mothers breastfeed started when I trained as a midwife in the late 1970s. In those days, few mothers breastfed their babies and mums who were bottle feeding were given an injection to stop them producing milk. Fortunately, this practice has stopped, which is good, as I know new mums can change their mind after a few days. That was 34 years ago, but I still remember a heartwarming story about Tina: she was a young teenage mother who was giving her baby up for adoption. Tina was bottle feeding her baby and doing all the care while she was in hospital. On the fourth day, she started to produce her breast milk and decided to breastfeed, which was successful as her baby boy took to breastfeeding without any problems. I cannot remember the outcome, but I thought she made the right decision. During my years as a health visitor, I was able to encourage and support mums to breastfeed for much longer. When mothers are in harmony with their baby, the experience of breastfeeding is positive and long lasting.

The following are my observations and first hand experience of the behavioural patterns of breastfed babies. Breastfeeding has many positive benefits for both mum and baby and is the natural, perfect food for babies. However, mothers can have a negative experience of breastfeeding, which may occur if the baby develops the habit of feeding to sleep and using the nipple as a dummy. Babies with this habit wake frequently through the night to comfort suck. Dads have a difficult time too. Their parental role is diminished, as the baby only wants mummy. Most of my emails are from mums whose babies have a breastfeeding-sleep association, so I have assigned a whole chapter just to breastfed babies.

**In this chapter:**

- Breastfeeding patterns
- Increasing milk supply
- How to introduce a multi-sensory sleep approach
- How to stop your baby breastfeeding to sleep during the day
- How to stop your baby breastfeeding to sleep at bedtime
- How to stop your baby breastfeeding to sleep during the night
- Frequently asked questions for breastfeeding

## Establishing breastfeeding

The first two weeks are crucial to the establishment of breastfeeding and mother-baby bonding. The sucking mechanism stimulates the production of the milk hormone, prolactin. Correct positioning at the breast is essential for successful breastfeeding; always seek help and guidance to ensure your baby is latched on correctly, as good attachment equals good milk production. Mothers who want to breastfeed, but are unable to latch their baby to the breast, are advised to start expressing their milk.

# Breastfeeding patterns

## Newborn babies

Full term, healthy babies alternate a feeding and sleeping pattern between midnight and midday; during the next 12 hours, babies are active and stay awake for longer between feeds. It is perfectly normal for babies to 'catnap' and 'cluster feed' all evening. Most babies are unsettled, restless and fidgety every evening from 5pm until midnight. Breastfed babies generally sleep well from midnight until 4am. Breastfed babies feed on demand and will feed up to eight times a day, each feed lasting approximately 30-40 minutes; in fact, most of their day is spent in a sleepy, milky haze. By age two to three weeks, most healthy, well-nourished babies have regained their birth weight. If this is not the case, seek support and advice from your midwife, health visitor, NCT or local breastfeeding support groups.

### Increasing milk supply

By the time babies are three months old, breastfeeding is established. Babies are alert and latch onto the nipple with minimal help. Some hungry babies can empty one breast in less than 10 minutes. Offer both breasts per feed to ensure prolactin levels remain high. Babies' appetites increase as they grow and one breast is not enough; one breast per feed is perfect for newborns, but by the time they are a month old, most babies require both breasts per feed.

### Advantages of offering both breasts after one month:

- Ensures adequate production of prolactin
- Discourages small, frequent snack feeds
- Increases the baby's stomach capacity to hold more milk
- Prevents babies from using the breast for sleepy feeds
- Reduces negative sleep association with breastfeeding
- Babies learn how to self-settle and sleep to their full age related potential

## Up to three months

Newborn babies are slow to feed initially, and tire easily. They average 30-40 minutes per feed and appear to be asleep for most of the feed and feed up to eight times a day. You will be advised to offer one breast per feed. After four weeks, breastfeeding is established; baby's appetite has increased and he can feed quicker. Your baby has regained birth weight and is gaining four to six ounces each week. This is a good time to offer the other breast as it increases the production of prolactin. Some women have greater production of milk and will only ever give one breast per feed. The majority of women will need to offer both breasts per feed. Always check and massage your breast before swapping to the other side.

## Three to six months

Three-month-old babies are efficient feeders. They can attach themselves to the breast very easily and empty your breast in 15 minutes if they are hungry enough. Avoid sleepy feeds, as this is how comfort sucking starts. Aim to feed after a sleep, not before. Most breastfed babies demand to be fed three-hourly during the day and can go for eight hours without a milk feed at night. To prevent a milk-sleep association, give the last milk feed in the lounge before the bath.

## Six to nine months

After six months of age, babies start to be weaned, though breast milk is their main food. This is a good time to give breastfeeds and solid food as part of the meal. Offer the breast before solid food if you are practising baby-led weaning, otherwise breastfeed after solid food. Mealtimes are 8am, midday, 4pm and 7.30pm. Avoid feeding your baby when he is tired, and also avoid offering the breast as a snack between meals. Breast milk is a complete food, not a drink. If you worry that your baby is thirsty, offer water in a sippy cup. If they are thirsty, they will drink it. Babies can sleep for 8-10 hours without needing milk feeds.

194

### Nine months to a year

This is the age when babies take less breast milk and more solid food; they still have one or two breastfeeds a day. If your baby has breast milk as part of his mealtime, he will naturally wean himself off the breast. It is usually babies who have a milk-sleep association that breastfeed for longer than a year, as they are using the breast for comfort sucking and sleep.

## How to introduce a multi-sensory sleep approach

I recommend introducing my Multi-Sensory Sleep Techniques and Routines from birth. A scented comforter, a soft, red glowing night light and soothing sounds of nature are relaxing at sleep time. They do not interfere with breastfeeding in any way. Breastfeeding to sleep is perfectly normal for a newborn baby. However, if breastfeeding to sleep continues for months, it prevents babies reaching their full sleep potential. My Multi-Sensory Approach to sleep and settling routines helps breastfed babies to reach their sleep potential.

### How to stop your baby breastfeeding to sleep during the day

The first step is to separate sleepy snack feeds from milk feeds. Tired babies do not feed properly. Within minutes, they fall asleep at the breast and wake up soon after, still hungry and tired; this behaviour can go on for the whole of the nap. Instead of feeding, take your baby out in the pram or car for a nap and only feed when your baby is alert and active, preferably 10 minutes after a sleep. Plan to breastfeed three-hourly (both breasts) during the day.

### Breastfeeding after a sleep provides the following advantages:

- Improves feeding technique
- Increases the time between breastfeeds
- Increases prolactin levels and milk production

- Establishes baby-led sleep
- Prevents comfort sleepy feeds

**How to stop your baby breastfeeding to sleep at bedtime**

When your baby can nap without breastfeeding, plan to do this at bedtime too: give the last breastfeed 15 minutes before the bath. Babies over seven months can have cereal or yogurt instead of a breastfeed. Follow the Multi-Sensory Sleep Routine for your baby's age and, in three or four days, your baby will self-settle to sleep without a breastfeed, which will dramatically improve your baby's ability to sleep without waking. The sleep potential for a six-month-old baby is seven to eight hours. A nine-month-old can sleep for 10 hours without waking for a feed.

**How to stop your baby breastfeeding to sleep during the night**

Follow the Multi-Sensory Sleep Routine for your baby's age. If your baby still needs milk during the night, breastfeed in dim light with the minimum of intervention; feed your baby until drowsy and then put your baby back down in the cot. Babies will naturally wean themselves off breast milk once they stop feeding to sleep and using the breast for comfort snacks during the day. Now daddy, and the rest of the family, can share bedtimes and you can relax in peace! Enjoy your night off.

## Frequently asked questions for breastfeeding

**Q. I am breastfeeding my three-week-old baby, but I want to be flexible and give my baby some of my expressed milk in a bottle. When is the best time to introduce this?**

**A.** If you are a new mum, don't start expressing until your baby is four weeks old, to ensure breastfeeding is established and you are feeling confident about it. The best time to express your milk is after the first feed in the morning, between 6am and 8am. Use a manual, battery operated or electric breast pump. Save the milk in the fridge and either use it within two to three days, or freeze it the same day it was expressed. Breastfed babies like a soft teat, so choose a brand that specialises in a breast/bottle style. The best time to give a breastfed baby a bottle of warmed, expressed milk is in the evening anytime from 8-11pm. This is a good time for dads to be involved in the feeding. The best time to breastfeed your baby is after you have had three or four hours sleep between midnight and 4am. This is when prolactin levels are high. You have had a good sleep and your baby will have a good feed.

**Q. My seven-month-old baby is fully breastfed and has started to take some solid food. I am going back to work in a month and want to stop breastfeeding and introduce formula in a bottle before I start work. When shall I make the switch?**

**A.** Most mums can continue to give one or two breastfeeds when they return to work, but if you want to stop breastfeeding, do it gradually to prevent engorgement and mastitis. Start to reduce the number of breastfeeds you give your baby two or three weeks before you return to work. The first breastfeed to stop is the lunchtime feed. Offer solid food and milk from a bottle or beaker. Allow your breasts to adjust to the change and, after a few days, stop another breastfeed at 7.30-8 pm. Offer milk in a bottle. If you feel your breasts are uncomfortable and engorged, express some milk until they feel comfortable. After a week, you will still be breastfeeding at approximately 6am, 10am and 4pm. The next feed to stop is the 10am breastfeed, then, three or four days later, the 4pm. Stop the last feed when you are ready.

**Q. My baby is four months old, fully breastfed and refuses to take a bottle or a dummy. How can I get her to take a bottle?**

**A.** The best way to encourage a four-month-old to take a bottle is to offer warmed, expressed milk in a bottle designed for breastfed babies. Wait until baby is hungry for a feed and get someone else to feed her, to prevent her from getting confused as to why you are not breastfeeding. She has to learn to suck in a new way as sucking a teat is very different to sucking your nipple. If you offer the bottle at bedtime every day, she will quickly learn how to suck the teat. Never force or pressurise her to suck the teat. That is counterproductive and will produce a negative association to the teat and bottle. With gentle perseverance, she will accept the bottle and take a small feed from it.

**Q. I think my baby is using my breast as a dummy. He is seven months old, on the 75 percentile for weight. I feed him three to four times in the night and five times during the day. I am exhausted. How can I stop this?**

**A.** Your baby is feeding like a newborn, and at seven months old, he is more than capable of sleeping for six hours without being fed. Breastfed babies are more likely to use the breast for comfort and sleep than bottle fed babies. Even breastfeeding mums can misjudge communicating effectively with their baby; popping babies on the breast for every whiny cry is not an appropriate response because babies can become completely dependent on the nipple for comfort and sleep.

1   Separate comfort breast feeds from milk feeds.

2   Aim to feed three-hourly during the day and as soon your baby uses the breast as a dummy, detach your baby – the feed is over.

3   When your baby is rubbing his eyes and yawning, instead of feeding, take your baby out for a short nap in the car or pram and when he wakes up, offer a breastfeed.

4   Introduce a comforter impregnated with your scent.

5   Aim to settle your baby in the nursery for at least one day nap without feeding.

6   Give your baby the last breastfeed before the bath, not after.

7   If your baby wakes before six hours, resettle him without a feed. Be flexible, as your baby might have a growth spurt (not every night, though).

8   Offer a milk feed if your baby wakes up after six hours.

# Chapter twelve

# What to expect when baby number two arrives

*"I noticed that parents with a three-year gap
seemed less harassed and more relaxed."*

One of the pleasures and privileges of working in the same town for 26 years was revisiting families with their second, third and even fourth baby. By the time I retired from health visiting, I was visiting mums who were babies at the start of my career. I could not believe the parents were old enough to have a baby until I made a quick calculation and realised that they were 26 years old – not too young at all! The perfect age to have their first baby. Where had all those years gone?

### When to have another baby

During my career, I was asked many times, *"When is the best time to have another baby?"* Midwives would often joke with new parents and, upon discharge from the maternity unit, say, *"See you next year!"* There is no ideal age to have another baby and second babies come along when you least expect it. Some couples like to have a year or two between their children and one mum preferred seven years between her children. It is a very personal choice; however, I noticed that parents with a three-year gap seemed less harassed and more relaxed. In my view, and from personal experience, most three-year-olds are more independent and able to do more for themselves: they can dress, walk confidently and feed themselves; most are toilet trained, which helps when there is a new baby to look after too. In addition, three-year-olds attend play group three to five sessions a week, which gives mums more time to spend with their new baby. I have personal experience of coping with a toddler and a new baby as my children were born on the same day, exactly 2 years and 35 minutes apart. It was hard work, demanding 'two babies on the knee' but I loved every minute and, for some reason, when I had my second, I felt like a proper mummy!

All young children are perceptive to subtle change and differences, they might notice you are different, but not understand why. This can lead to separation anxiety, sleep and toilet training regression, food refusal and increased temper tantrums.

**In this chapter:**

- Toddler still sleeping in your bed
- Preparing your toddler for the new baby
- New baby sleep problems
- How to prevent new baby sleep problems
- How to manage your baby and toddler at bedtime
- Bedtime routine for baby and toddler

### Toddler still sleeping in your bed

I receive emails from mums, usually late in their pregnancy, desperately seeking sleep advice for their toddler who is still sleeping in their bed. They are anxious to resolve their toddlers' sleeping problem before the birth. My Multi-Sensory Sleep Routines are perfect for toddlers and, within three to four days of introducing them, your toddler will be sleeping in their own bed.

### How to prepare your toddler for the arrival of a new brother or sister

Depending on your toddler's awareness and language development, you can explain in simple terms what is going to happen. Allow your child to make the first noticing comment; some toddlers are interested and ask lots of questions. It is unnecessary to go into great detail as very few children are interested or understand long explanations. Here is a sweet story: *second-time mum-to-be, Hilary, asked her three-year-old son, James, whether he would like a baby sister or baby brother. He replied he would like a monkey! A few weeks later, Hilary came to baby clinic holding her new baby girl and James walked in, looking very proud and pleased with himself, holding his new cuddly toy monkey!*

### Toddler adjusting to the new baby

The arrival of a new brother or sister can destabilise home life for a few weeks and this is a period of adjustment for all the family. To prevent jealousies, involve your toddler in as much baby care as is appropriate for their age and development. It helps your toddler to adjust to the new baby if your toddler's daily routine remains the same. In my experience, family and friends are very supportive and willingly take toddlers to their music, dancing classes and toddler groups. Children like their daily routine and it reassures them that their world is the same and you are still their mummy.

# New baby sleep problems

"If he was my first, I wouldn't have had any more!" I have heard this comment many times; how parents cope with their new addition depends entirely on how well they managed with their first child. What I discovered was the new baby had a very different personality to their older sibling and what worked with their first child was not working second time round. I know feeling helpless and confused undermines parents' confidence and many feel embarrassed, feeling that they should know what to do. Every child is an individual with different personality traits; most siblings have the completely opposite temperament and nature. Some babies are easier to look after than other babies: they are naturally relaxed and easy to look after, they feed well and drift off to sleep with the minimum of fuss; then there are the babies I have described in previous chapters, who have sensitive natures, sensitive to any change in their environment and many suffer from reflux and colic. Inevitably, those babies will be predisposed to developing a sleeping problem.

Some new babies adapt to a busy household and don't appear to have a sleeping problem, while others do. Here is a list of problems I have encountered:

1   The baby slots into the siblings activities and daily routine so that he does not get a chance to have quality day naps in the cot.

2   Exposure to over-stimulating environments such as toddler groups (not suitable for newborns) makes them unable to relax and self-soothe at sleep times.

3   Sleeping in the car seat becomes the norm for daytime naps.

4   The baby never plays in their nursery and goes in the cot asleep, never awake.

5   The baby spends most of his waking time in the siblings' bedrooms.

6   The bedtime routine is fitted around the older child/children and the baby's routine, therefore, slot into the siblings' bedtime routine.

7   Mum spends so much of her time rushing to meet the needs of her older children, her baby does not get the chance for proper feeds, is constantly snacking at the breast and uses the breast for comfort and sleep.

None of the above need concern you if your baby is sleeping to their sleep potential. However, in my experience, this is rarely the case.

### How to prevent new baby sleep problems

It is important that your new baby becomes an accepted part of the family, so attending toddler groups with your newborn is inevitable. To reduce stimulation overload, choose a quiet corner to feed where your baby can sleep in relative peace.

Make a conscious decision to spend quality playtime and quiet time with your baby in their bedroom, aim to do this before a day nap and just before bath time.

To prevent your baby using the breast for comfort and sleep, I recommend you separate your breast milk feeds from comfort sleepy feeds. Babies over three months old can be fed three-hourly and do not need to snack at the breast near a sleep time, instead, avoid sleepy feeds and feeding to sleep. Feed your baby when he wakes up from a day nap, not before. Offer your baby both breasts per feed to increase the stomach capacity to hold more milk; you cannot overfeed breastfed babies.

It is inevitable your baby or toddler will have a nap in the car on the school run, but short cat naps are not energising enough and babies appear constantly tired. The best way to deal with this problem is to wake your baby after the journey and then wait a few hours until your baby is tired again. Wait for the tired signs and plan to settle your baby in the cot for a longer day nap before you head out again.

Although each change might seem insignificant and subtle, combining them can make a positive impact on your baby's sleeping potential.

## How to manage your baby and toddler at bedtime

Bedtime can be quite hectic with only one child to consider, so getting more than one child ready for bed can be challenging, especially if you manage bedtime on your own. Many parents rush bedtime and it becomes a chore. It is natural to want the children in bed as quickly as possible; parents are desperate to sit down, have a meal, relax and spend childfree time together before their own bedtime. Whether you are at home with your children, working full or part time, you are a busy mum! There is such a lot to do before bedtime: nursery or school pick up, after school activities, a quick visit to the super market, homework, and tea to prepare – all before bedtime.

**Poor quality sleep increases risk of postnatal depression**

Looking after more than one child requires good health, lots of energy and stamina. If you are not getting at least six to seven solid hours of sleep at night, your health and wellbeing could be compromised. Poor quality and broken sleep exacerbate the risk of postnatal depression, which can occur at any time in the first year of birth. Therefore, slow the pace down and implement my Multi-Sensory Sleep Techniques and Sleep Routines for your baby and toddler

# Bedtime routine for baby and toddler

From three months old, most babies will be ready for bed by 8pm, aim to synchronise your baby's and toddler's bedtime routines. The following sequence is for babies and toddlers that have made positive sleep associations. This is a prerequisite before commencing my sleep routine:

- Both children spend sensory playtime in their nursery/ bedroom
- Both children have a sleep teddy/comforter, night light and soothing music at sleep time
- Both children can sleep to their maximum age related sleep potential
- Both children can self-settle to sleep with minimum parental intervention
- Your baby has a day nap in the cot

If this is not the case, solve each sleep problem first before trying to synchronise the bedtime routines.

**This is the routine to follow for babies and toddlers who go to sleep at 8pm:**

 Spend quiet play time in the lounge 20 minutes before bath time.

 Give your baby a last milk feed (breast/bottle) in the lounge and offer your toddler supper before the bath.

 Go up to your baby's room and switch on the sensory lights, mobile and music, play, chat and interact with your baby and toddler for 5-10 minutes, then leave your baby in their cot looking at the mobile while you set up your toddler's bedroom.

 With your toddler, switch on the night light, music (optional) and let your toddler choose their book to read; leave dummy/comforter/sleep teddy in the bedroom.

 Take your toddler with you while you run the bath.

 Bathe the children together, if you feel your baby is too young, bath them separately.

 Dress the children in the bathroom if you have enough space, close the bathroom door to prevent your toddler running about and if you have help at bath-time, dress the children separately in their own rooms.

 Walk your toddler to your baby's room and settle your baby first, switching the lights to a soft, red glow and playing sea sounds; leave your baby for 5-10 minutes while you settle your toddler into their bed and read the story.

 Once your toddler is settled, return to your baby and switch off the lights and sleep music.

From start to finish the whole routine should not take more than 45 minutes. Babies and toddlers like a structured bedtime routine, they remember the sequence and anticipate what comes next. Babies and toddlers under the age of three to four years are too young to cope with changes in the bedtime routine and the actual time you start the routine is not significant, it is the flow of the sequence that is important.

# Chapter thirteen

# What to expect when you have twins

*"Identical twins have different personalities; in my experience, one twin is generally more outgoing and independent than the other."*

If you are reading this chapter, you have had twins – congratulations! Now the fun begins. The chance of having twins is one in ninety pregnancies. The small town where I worked as a health visitor for 26 years was renowned for twins. In one year, I visited 20 sets of twins and a set of triplets!

I think every couple who goes to the hospital for the first scan will be wondering if the scan will show they are expecting twins. How did you feel when you were told you were going to have twins: shocked, amazed, stunned, panicked, thrilled? Plunged into a nightmare? Or in a nanosecond, did you experience every human emotion? A mum recently told me she felt privileged to have twins. If you have a toddler and newborn twins, your life is going to be very busy and you can feel pulled in all directions. There is the added worry of the twins being born premature and all that entails. In my experience, most parents have a mixture of emotions, unless they are one of a pair of twins themselves, in which case, twin parents often assume they will have twins, hope they will have twins and are, indeed, a little disappointed if they do not have twins!

As an observer, I am fascinated by twins. I have noticed that even though the babies share and experience so much together, each will respond and interact differently to the world around them. Even identical twins have different personalities; in my experience, one twin is generally more outgoing and more independent than the other.

**In this chapter:**

- The nursery
- Multi-sensory sleep techniques for twins
- Feeding routines for twins
- Bedtime routine
- How to respond to your twins during the night
- What to do when one twin wakes the other
- What to do when twins don't want to sleep together
- When to move twins to the nursery

**Support**

Looking after twins takes up much more time and energy than looking after one baby; everything takes twice as long, so if you receive offers of help, take them. Share the workload and share the pleasure and delight of looking after two babies. If your partner is your only support, when he goes back to work, you will be on our own for most of the day, so what will you do when your babies are crying at the same time? This will be an everyday occurrence and very stressful for even the most experienced and organised parent. Which baby do you pick up first? Will it be the baby that has the loudest cry? Being organised and having some routines in place will help with stressful dilemmas. It can be a few months before some mums feel confident to go out. Social media such as Facebook and Twitter have many support groups for parents of twins and they are a great way to get advice and support without the stress and worry of leaving the house with two new babies. However, once you feel ready, you can get help and support from and attend twins clubs in most towns and cities.

### Other children

If you have older children, they, too, will be fascinated and want to be involved, so allow them to participate as much as is appropriate for their age. While the twins are asleep in your bedroom, spend quality time with your older children to prevent resentment and jealousies developing.

### Routines

Routines should be based on what feels natural for you and common sense. Avoid strict, rigid, impractical routines that take over your life as they can undermine your natural parenting ability. Following very strict daytime and bedtime routines, based on set times, is unnatural for babies and can set you up to fail; some parenting books are unrealistic and too harsh. My approach to baby routines is baby-led, baby-friendly and parent-empowering. Sleep and baby routines are a balance between what feels right for you and what your babies are capable of.

## The nursery

### Equipment

Twins come with two of everything: cots, Moses baskets, changing mats, reclining chairs, car seats etc. Until you have time to adjust to the change in your life, it is easier to keep all baby equipment and baby paraphernalia handy: the best place is the nursery or your bedroom.

### Bedroom set up

I recommend that for the first six weeks, you set up your bedroom or the nursery to be a day room for your babies. Babies spend the first six weeks in a sleepy, milky haze, so the nursery or your bedroom has the best atmosphere for sleep and relaxation, make it as comfortable and as practical as possible for yourself and your babies as you will be spending many hours during the day just feeding and changing. Buy a practical changing table that has drawers for storing nappies and clothes. If you can fit two cots in your bedroom, then set up the cots ready and place the Moses baskets inside the cots; however, there are other varieties of cots and bassinets to choose from, so pick one that suits your needs. Now the nursery or bedroom is ready, set up the baby monitor to give you added peace of mind.

### Sensory overload

Babies are born with a heightened sense of smell and hearing, therefore every smell and sound in your home is a new sensation and your babies are prone to becoming overstimulated and overtired; let them adjust to their home environment gradually. Initially, keep the babies close to you during the day and use your bedroom for day naps, as this is where they sleep at night and the room will have a familiar, comforting smell, reminding your babies of you.

# Multi-sensory sleep techniques for twins

Maternal stress, worry and postnatal depression can become exacerbated by lack of sleep. Therefore, introducing your babies to my Multi-Sensory Sleep Techniques from day one will ensure your babies make natural sleep associations with smell, sound, sight, touch and taste. Within days, natural sleep associations will quickly become familiar and reassuring for your babies.

### Positive sleep associations:

### Sight

Attach a colourful mobile to the cot (see Rainforest Mobile in chapter three). Mobiles develop eye coordination and keep babies entertained for at least 10-15 minutes at a time. If you thought a mobile is too stimulating at sleep time, this is not the case: the mobile is entertaining your babies, giving them something of interest to focus and stare at until they are ready for sleep. Avoid bland, wind up mobiles as babies find them very boring and uninteresting.

A positive sleep association is made with the cot, the nursery and the mobile so the whole experience for babies is relaxed, calm and pleasurable. Lights fascinate all new babies and they will gaze intently at interesting bright lights. To make the nursery more appealing for young babies, darken the room and use a night light that changes colour or projects patterns on the walls or ceiling: make it 'womb like with stars'.

### Sound

Choose a mobile that plays soothing nature sounds or classical music, as they are relaxing and calming for babies. Play a different sound for different activities, for example, play music that is upbeat and lively at nappy changing time; change the music to something more relaxing during a feed, when your babies are relaxing and ready to sleep, play soothing, repetitive nature sounds and ocean waves. You can also play the music you listened to during your pregnancy; your babies will recognise it and enjoy listening to it again. Even Jon Bon Jovi! Though not at sleep time...

### Smell/Touch

Introduce your babies to a teddy or comforter as soon as possible after birth. Pop a comforter down your bra during feeding and then attach one to each cot at sleep time, close enough for your babies to smell it. Once babies have made positive sleep attachments to a teddy/comforter they continue to sleep well, even after their vaccinations, teething, colds and tummy upsets. After age three months, it is safe to leave a comforter in each cot, where your babies can hold them as they sleep. I have watched babies search for their comforter in light sleep, and once they have located it, snuggle up to it and drift back off to sleep again.

### Senses to avoid

While babies are sleeping, their environment and ambience needs to be stable and regulated, so avoid noisy areas or cooking smells permeating into the room, as they will disturb your sleeping babies.

## Taste

Babies aged up to six months have a strong desire to suck and once they are satisfied during a feed they stop sucking. If babies have a dummy, use the breast for comfort, or have sleepy feeds, they develop a sleep-taste attachment to the breast/bottle/dummy, which is more difficult to break as babies get older. Most breastfeeding twin mums are unable to indulge their babies' preference for non-nutritive sucking and keep breastfeeding just for nutrition not comfort. This approach helps babies to self-regulate their milk intake and prevents babies using the breast for sleep.

# *Feeding routines for twins*

Rita, an experienced mum of twins, said the easiest way to manage and cope with twins was to synchronise feeding and sleeping patterns – excellent advice. Rita did not like waking the sleeping twin, but it was the only way she could synchronise feed/sleep patterns.

## Breastfeeding

Breastfeeding twins simultaneously takes time and practice; your midwife will show you how to position the babies so they and you are comfortable. Rita said it was easier and quicker to breastfeed her twins in tandem; she was a second time mum and had breastfed before, but even with previous experience, she needed help with initial attachment. Breastfeeding twins does take a bit more practice to get the positioning right and, initially, she needed help fixing them at the breast. She also said how amazed she was that the babies seemed to know they were about to be fed and would wait patiently for their turn.

### When one twin refuses to feed at the breast

Fiona was breastfeeding her twins, a boy and a girl. Her baby boy was eager to feed and fed well at the breast, but her baby girl could not latch on correctly and after lots of help and several frustrating days she decided to bottle feed her and breastfeed her baby boy. This must have been a difficult decision to make, as breast milk contains antibodies that boost babies' immune systems and is the perfect food for babies. The ideal solution would be to express milk so that both babies benefit from breast milk.

### Bottle feeding

If you are bottle feeding, aim to either feed your babies at the same time or split the feed into four halves: twin one has half a feed and then sits in the reclining chair, sucking a dummy, (if you are using one) while twin two has half a feed, then swap them over. If they are crying for milk at the same time, feed while they sit in reclining chairs and lift them out individually to wind. If you struggle to get their wind up, let them suck a dummy while you wind as the sucking action relaxes babies and releases the wind.

## Bedtime routine

This is the sequence to follow when your babies are three months old and are normally asleep by 8pm. Aim to let your babies have an afternoon nap and wake them up after 4pm. If your babies have either a comforter/sleep teddy/dummy, leave them in the nursery for sleep times only.

### 7pm Quiet playtime

Spend 10-15 minutes in the lounge. Turn off the TV and play some relaxing music, which will signal to your babies that the sleep routine has commenced.

Sit, read and play quietly with your babies.

### 7.15pm Last milk feed

Give the last milk feed breast/bottle in the lounge

before the bath. Babies do not need large quantities of milk to sleep well at night. If the twins are over six months old and weaned, offer cereal and mashed banana, or a dairy-free substitute if they are milk intolerant, instead of a milk feed.

### 7.30pm Sensory playtime

Take your babies up to their bedrooms and switch on the fairy lights/light show/mobile/music. This is sensory playtime and a fun time in the nursery. Sit and read or chat to your babies, or if they are old enough, sit them in the cot with some toys. Lamaze sensory toys make ideal cot toys (pictured in chapter six). While the babies are safe in their cots, run the bath and collect their nightclothes.

### 7.45pm Bath fun time

Bath your babies together. If you are doing bath time on your own, lie the babies down in shallow bath water up to the level of their ears. Let them kick, stretch, splash and play. Once they have had enough bath time, dress the babies in the bathroom ready for bed. Stop using a sleeping bag if your babies can crawl or pull to stand as they could easily trip, fall and hurt themselves.

### 8pm Sleep time

Carry the babies straight back to their cot and lie them down. They do not need any more cuddles and kisses to help them sleep and they will have more tomorrow. If your babies can sit up, let them sit in the cot and play with a toy for a few minutes. Turn off all lights but keep a soft red glow light (such as the Slumber Buddy pictured in chapter three) and change the music to sea sounds, as they are more hypnotic than other sleep sounds. Now is the time to give your babies their comforter/sleep teddy. If you know your babies can self-settle, leave the room. If your babies prefer you to stay in the room, sit on the floor where they can see you; do not give eye contact, talk, and touch or interact with them. If they start to cry, give them the OK thumbs up sign and give the baby sign for sleep. If your babies are standing up, pat the mattress and say, "*Sleepy time. Lie down.*" Turn your back to avoid eye contact. Once your baby has settled down to sleep, turn off all music and lights.

**REM sleep cycle**

Babies are in light REM sleep at the start and end of their night sleep and during the day, therefore, during this time they are easily woken and disturbed so aim to keep their sleeping environment controlled and stable. However, babies that have learnt how to self-soothe relax into peaceful sleep, stay asleep, sleep to their sleep potential and only wake up for a feed.

**Age related sleep potential**

A baby's sleep potential is the unique number of hours an individual baby needs in a 24-hour period. I have discovered that most babies aged 12 months need 12 hours a day, with some needing a little more or less. If babies are encouraged to have long day naps, they will sleep less at night, so it is important that sleep is baby-led and babies are not coerced into day naps with cuddles, rocking and feeding to sleep. Babies who can self-soothe will sleep when they are ready and not before. I have met babies who refuse any day nap, but will sleep 12 hours at night. They are perfectly healthy and energetic, play all day – usually in case they miss something – and enjoy going to bed and sleeping all night. They wake up totally refreshed and ready to start another busy day.

# How to respond to your twins during the night

Babies over three months old can sleep for six to eight hours without waking. If your babies wake between midnight and 4am, offer a milk feed.

Babies over six months do not need milk during the night and most can sleep from 8pm until 4am without waking for a feed. Babies who have learned how to self-settle at bedtime will sleep to their unique age related sleep potential.

If your six-month-old babies wake only a few hours after the last feed, re-settle them with quiet distraction and avoid picking your babies out of the cot. Use the soft glow red lights if your babies are fully awake, and use the baby signing for sleep (place your hands together and at the side of your face).

### Teaching your babies to self-settle

Self-settling or self-soothing is the key to quality sleep, as sleep is the cornerstone of any daytime routine. Babies who can self-soothe are easier to look after. They settle to sleep easily during the day, which leads to quality day naps (an hour or longer), as opposed to short, 20-minute catnaps (great for cats, not for babies).

### Advantage of self-settling

Babies wake up refreshed and eager to feed. After a good feed, babies are generally content for about 30 minutes and more inclined to sit, look about and interact with their world without needing constant attention. Very young babies have a short attention span and get bored after 15 minutes; therefore, they will require more attention and entertaining. Contented babies sleep well, feed well and consequently will free up some time for you!

If your babies are cuddled or fed to sleep, they do not know how to self-settle, so this use distraction technique.

### Distraction technique

All babies sound frustrated and unhappy when they learn how to self-settle for the first time. This is a new experience for your baby, so empathise and understand how difficult this is for them to do this; make the process as easy for your baby as possible. Patience, persistence and gentle perseverance is the key to my approach.

Parents hate to see their baby crying. Before babies start their 'tired baby cry' they can sound frustrated and angry. I have heard this cry in very young babies and the best way to stop it is to distract your baby before the cry escalates into a hysterical cry.

To reduce unnecessary crying, use my distraction techniques, depending on your babies' personalities, which is easy to do: tap the side of the cot, click your fingers, move the Slumber Buddies lights about the nursery or gently shake a rattle to get your babies' attention. Once you have stopped your babies' cries, stop the distraction immediately. Reassure them with positive praise, use baby thumbs up sign for OK and make the sign for sleep. Babies as young as five months old recognise this sign and will understand what you are doing.

Some older babies are not impressed by magic shows and need more distraction. VTech toys, like Alfie Bear, or books that play nursery rhymes or animal noises are very effective at distracting an older baby. Place a VTech toy, or something similar, in the cot and switch it on for a second or two; leave the toys in the cot and let your babies distract themselves and press the buttons. Choose the toys your babies like to play with during the day: one couple I knew let their babies play with some musical toys, toy piano and drum kit. They might play in the cot for 5-10 minutes before they are ready to settle down ready to sleep.

Once your babies are truly tired and ready to self-settle, the cry changes to a low volume whine, a low cry with lots of yawns and eye rubs. This is the self-settling cry and they are minutes from sleep. Do not distract or intervene; give them the time and opportunity to self-settle. Once they have learned how to self-settle, they will need to practise this technique five or six more times before it becomes a habit, after which your baby will not need any you or any distraction at sleep time and will settle down to sleep very contentedly and without a peep.

### What to do when one twin wakes the other twin

Identical twins tend to have a similar sleep potential but non-identical twins are unique and have different sleep potentials. I noticed this behaviour in one-year-old, non-identical twin boys: one boy liked a dummy (Adam) and the other a comforter (Aidan).

The twin with the comforter slept better that the twin with the dummy, because when Adam lost his dummy during the night, he stood up crying in his cot and expected mum and dad to find it for him, waking Aiden at the same time. This pattern would go on repeatedly throughout the night, leaving both parents exhausted and exasperated with two grumpy babies to care for the next day.

The solution to this problem was to reduce Adam's dependency on the dummy. His parents:

- Used the dummy for sleep times only
- Taught Adam to search for his dummy and put it back in himself by placing the dummy in the cot and patting her hand around to find it, encouraging him to get it
- Lying on the floor by his cot to role-play sleep, yawning and snoring and waiting until Adam decided to reach for his dummy, lie down and go to sleep

Within two to three days, Adam understood what was expected of him and consequently he was sleeping through the night. Mum sometimes heard him wake and search for his dummy until he found it himself. It was the sensible approach to teach Adam to be as independent as possible. If babies have reached a stage of development when they are physically able to reach for toys and take them to their mouth, then the same principle applies to the dummy.

### What to do when twins don't want to sleep together

Although the babies share the same womb for nine months, do not naturally assume that your babies will want to continue sleeping together. This was very evident during a home visit I made to Lisa, a mum with 10-day-old twins, a boy and a girl. The baby boy wanted to snuggle in close to his sister, but she wriggled away from him and settled when she had her own space, she did not want him next to her anymore. Lisa had planned to keep them in the same cot, but respected the individual needs of her babies. It would have been unfair to the baby girl to allow her brother to invade her space.

Some babies want more cuddles than other. Babies and twins are no exception: to provide the close comfort her baby boy preferred, we replicated the feeling of being cuddled by positioning two very soft 10-inch teddies either side of him.

Additionally, to help her baby boy to settle, Lisa used Ewan the Dream Sheep, a sleep toy: she positioned it near enough so that he could see the soft glowing light and hear the womb sounds. This worked incredibly well. Previously, he had been fractious and Lisa could not put him down without him crying, but within a few minutes of watching the light and listening to the heartbeat, he relaxed and went to sleep. As soon as both babies were asleep, we removed the teddies and sleep toy. Sleep toys are useful sleep aids, they help babies to relax, settle to sleep and become positive sleep associations.

### When to move twins to the nursery

Twins grow just as fast as singletons and often need to go into a cot sooner than their mums prefer. I remember seeing eight-week-old twins sharing a cot. They looked cute and cosy together, but they were kicking each other and waking each other up. Once they were in their own cot, their sleeping potential improved dramatically.

Alice, their mum, then faced a new challenge: the two cot beds did not fit in her bedroom so the babies needed to go into the nursery. Her only option was to create a nursery environment that was soothing, comforting and relaxing. Alice spent quality time in the nursery, playing with them, reading stories, singing and playing classical music, feeding and changing and within days, the room was familiar to the babies and they were having day naps in there, too. When Alice saw how contented and relaxed they looked sleeping in their own cots, she settled them to sleep in the nursery at night and in her words, *"never looked back"*.

If you have not found the answer to your sleep problem, I recommend you read the chapter specific to your baby's age and look in Chapter 16, frequently asked questions, on page 253.

# Chapter fourteen

# What to expect with babies with health problems

*"The majority of my sleep referrals are for babies who either have had gastro oesophageal reflux or still have it."*

While I was researching for this book, I found a report that said parents were more concerned about their baby's sleep problem than a medical problem. From a heath visiting perspective, I believe the two are related, as medical problems can significantly disturb a baby's sleeping pattern. Parents, naturally, want to comfort, cuddle and soothe their distressed baby to sleep. However, after a period of between three and six months, most feeding problems have been resolved, while babies have become reliant on cuddles or need to be fed to sleep. Most of my referrals are from mums whose babies initially had a feeding problem and now have a behavioural sleeping problem.

My Multi-Sensory Sleep Techniques and Sleep Routines are perfect for babies with the following medical conditions:

- Gastro oesophageal reflux
- Milk allergy and milk intolerance
- Eczema
- Teething
- Colds and viruses

# Gastro oesophageal reflux

The majority of my sleep referrals are for babies who either have had gastro oesophageal reflux (GOR) or still have it. It is very common in babies from birth to nine months and both of my children had it until they could sit up. However, the good news is that babies with reflux can sleep just as well as babies who do not have reflux.

### What is GOR?

GOR is a common condition in young babies. The term reflux describes a condition when the contents of the stomach, known as a posset, are regurgitated either just after a feed or several hours afterwards. Undeveloped and immature lax oesophageal sphincter muscles cause the problem. The posset consistency changes depending on how long the milk has been in the stomach. As soon as milk enters the stomach, the acid contents of the stomach start to digest and break down the milk protein. A posset soon after a feed looks like thick milk. An hour later the posset is thick and curdled and after two or three hours, a posset looks like water with a few bits of curdled milk. GOR can vary from mild, moderate to severe.

### Mild GOR

Most babies seem to cope very well with mild GOR. They have normal weight gain and do not appear to be distressed when they burp or regurgitate the curdled milk. In a mild case of reflux, the baby will posset a mouthful of milk after every feed, usually with a burp. The best way to prevent regurgitation is to sit your baby up a couple of times during a feed and avoid vigorously patting and rubbing as this can increase the posset. Instead, sit your baby on your knee, support your baby's head under the chin and with your other hand, keep your baby's back as straight as possible. Your baby will sit on your knee quite comfortably in this position until the wind is released. After a good burp, your baby is ready to feed again.

Fortunately, the condition is self-limiting. By the time the baby is about a year old, the oesophageal sphincter matures, and the GOR symptoms reduce and eventually cease.

Until treatment is commenced or until the symptoms have reduced, parents are naturally concerned and anxious about their baby. Babies with reflux can feel uncomfortable after a feed, they can appear quite agitated, wave their arms about and arch their back, which looks distressing and mums naturally feel helpless and upset seeing their baby behave in such a way. Parents wonder whether their baby is experiencing pain, and this constant worry and anxiety causes many parents to develop ways of pacifying and comforting their baby to reduce the symptoms of reflux. Frequent cradling, rocking, patting and breastfeeding babies to sleep can often result in a sleeping problem long after the GOR symptoms have been resolved.

### Moderate GOR

In a moderate case of GOR, the posset is more than just a mouthful and the baby continues to posset until the next feed. It is rare that weight gain is affected by frequent possets, but curdled milk tastes bitter and I have seen babies pull a face in disgust as the regurgitated milk tastes sour. A dietician or GP will offer advice, as this type of reflux is often treated with a milk thickener and an antacid such as Gaviscon. Gaviscon protects the walls of the oesophagus from acidic reflux and it forms a viscous gel 'raft' that floats on the surface of the stomach contents, preventing reflux. Your GP will prescribe the appropriate medication for your baby.

### Silent reflux

Most babies with GOR regurgitate milk, but in the condition called 'silent reflux', some of the stomach contents pass through the oesophageal sphincter into the oesophagus but not as far as the mouth. Until treatment is prescribed, babies can be fast asleep, then grimace in pain and cry out in their sleep. This experience is very stressing for both baby and parents.

In severe cases of GOR, the baby's stomach contents are more acidic than normal and the baby feels a burning sensation. Babies with severe GOR symptoms are usually referred to paediatricians and medication is prescribed to alleviate the condition.

### How to prevent a posset after a feed

It helps to reduce posset if you feed your baby in an upright position and sit your baby in a chair for 30 minutes following a feed. During the night, it is not practical to sit for 30 minutes holding your baby, as your baby will fall asleep in your arms and wake up in the next sleep cycle. This is a very common sleeping problem, so follow these steps to prevent a sleeping problem from occurring in the first place:

- Lie your baby down after a night feed on a special sleeping mattress designed for babies with GOR
- Create a relaxing and sensory sleeping environment as this will dramatically improve your baby's ability to self-soothe, relax, calm and settle for a day nap and night sleep
- Promote positive sleep attachments to a comforter/soft teddy, a starry night light and nature sounds to enhance positive sleep associations and ensure your baby reaches their maximum sleep potential: your baby's sleep potential is the number of hours they can sleep without waking for a milk feed, either breast or bottle

# Milk allergy and lactose intolerance

### What is lactose intolerance?

Lactose intolerance is a common condition in bottle fed babies and occasionally breastfed babies. Mums regularly contact me for advice and support once it has been diagnosed by their GP. Lactose is the sugar part of milk and some young babies are unable to digest it properly. I noticed that most babies did not present with symptoms from birth; the condition was noticeable from two to three weeks after birth.

**The typical symptoms I noticed were:**

- Large, frothy, yellow stools (mousse like in consistency)
- The babies were very hungry and gulped down large feeds
- Babies' tummies were bloated and they passed excessive amounts of wind; one mum described her baby's nappies as explosive
- Quite often, the babies cried out in their sleep when they burped and trumped!

### How to treat lactose intolerance

Most GPs will test the stool before prescribing lactose free milk. Lactose intolerance is easy to treat and lactose-free formula milk is given to bottle fed babies; however, I noticed breastfed babies suffered from lactose intolerance, too. Their mums controlled the symptoms by changing their diet and swapping dairy products for rice, oat and soya milk instead.

After six months of age, most of the babies I observed were able to digest some lactose and their mums were able to wean their babies onto small amounts of cows' milk and dairy products. By the age of one year, their symptoms had resolved.

### Cows' milk allergy

A cows' milk allergy can be a very serious condition and very often hereditary. Mums I spoke to were either milk intolerant themselves or a family member was allergic to milk.

### Symptoms of milk allergy

The baby is allergic to the protein content of cow's milk and presents with any of the following:

- Projectile vomiting after milk
- Diarrhoea or constipation
- Dry red and inflamed skin or eczema
- Weight loss and failure to gain weight
- Inconsolable crying

Any of the above symptoms would be a cause of concern for any parent and once a diagnosis has been made by a consultant paediatrician, special milk-free formula is prescribed. The worst allergy I encountered was in a breastfed baby. After skin tests, his mum omitted cow's milk, cheese and yogurt from her diet and substituted calcium-enriched products such as rice and oat milk.

I recommend diagnosis and treatment before implementing my Multi-Sensory Sleep Techniques and Sleep Routines. However, a teddy/comforter, soft, starry red glow light, and soothing nature sounds at sleep times will help to de-stress, relax, and calm the babies.

# Eczema

## What is eczema?

In the UK, one in five children and one in twelve adults has eczema. Eczema is a genetic condition and, in most cases, there will be a family history of eczema, asthma or hay fever. Our skin provides a strong, effective barrier that protects the body from infection or irritation. If your baby has eczema, their skin may not produce as much fat and oil as other babies. Soap and bubble bath will remove oil from anyone's skin and scented bath products can irritate your baby's skin. When I was a health visitor, I ran an eczema clinic and was able to advise and prescribe over-the-counter prescriptions of emollients, bath oils and creams to treat the dry skin and eczema.

## When does eczema appear?

The mums that came to my clinic usually first noticed the condition when their baby was about ten- to twelve-weeks-old. I noticed that the eczema flared up during weaning and, in most cases, by 12 months had completely gone.

## Mild eczema

In its mildest form, eczema causes the skin to be dry, scaly, red and itchy. The baby's skin feels rough and dry to touch; there might be a few red dry patches on the face, abdomen, upper shoulder and outer thighs. Regular application of emollients and bath oils soften the skin and prevent flare-ups. If you take your baby swimming, apply a thin layer of cream before swimming and after the session, wash the chlorine off, and apply more cream.

## Moderate to severe eczema

In severe cases of eczema, the whole of the baby's body is dry, red and itchy and the baby is uncomfortable, distressed and constantly scratching.

Appropriate treatment and regular application of prescribed 1% Hydrocortisone instantly relieves inflammation and the itch, while bath oils and greasy creams soften and moisturise the skin. Your GP, practice nurse or health visitor will advise you on the correct amount to apply to your baby's skin.

## Eczema and sleep

It is important to treat eczema as it can disturb babies' sleep patterns, prevents babies from settling at bedtime and is the cause of frequent waking during the night. My Multi-Sensory Sleep Routines are perfect for babies with eczema. Although I advise a bath as part of the bedtime routine, some babies are itchy for an hour after their bath, in which case do not incorporate a bath into the bedtime routine.

# Teething

Parents worry about teething and its effect on their baby's sleeping pattern and many parents maintain teething is the cause of their sleepless nights. In my experience, babies who know how to self-soothe and self-settle seem to cope with teething and it does not affect their sleep. Here are some frequently asked teething questions.

## Q. When do babies start to teethe?

**A.** At birth, the first teeth are deep in the jaw bone and start to move up to the gum line from three months old. This is the age when parents notice their baby dribbling and rubbing their gums with their fist. Three-month-old babies have entered into a new phase of development. They have learned how to put their hands in their mouth and they produce more saliva in preparation for weaning. Babies continue to dribble and drool until two years of age or until their back molars have erupted. When babies are teething, they can look hot, flushed, whiny and have one red cheek. Just to complicate matters, the baby might also have a cold, with a runny nose and watery eyes, as babies can experience six consecutive colds in the first year of life. A mixture of symptoms can confuse parents and they worry more. My recommendation is parents first treat the symptoms their baby presents with. If their baby feels hot, give a drink of cool water and, to reduce the fever and ease any pain, give the recommended dose of Paracetamol or similar pain-relief for babies. Within 20 minutes, the symptoms should have resolved and your baby will be happy and content again.

## Q. When will I see the first tooth?

**A.** Very rarely, babies are born with a tooth but, on average, most babies have their first tooth by their first birthday. The first teeth are tiny, they have serrated edges and are very sharp. Most mums only notice their baby has a tooth when they are bitten! The bottom two teeth pop through first, followed by the top two teeth. From three months of age until two years, babies are, in effect, teething for nearly two years. It is a normal phase of development and most babies cope well with teething. It does not disturb their sleep if they already have a good sleep routine and can self-settle. However, those babies that need parental intervention at sleep times may have increased waking during teething.

## Q. What should I do if teething wakes my baby in the night?

**A.** Firstly, implement the Multi-Sensory Sleep Routine appropriate for your baby. Secondly, when your baby wakes in the night with the symptoms described above, treat the symptoms. Then sit together in the nursery for 20 minutes, look at the red glow light and listen to soothing ocean sea sounds. When the pain and discomfort has passed and your baby is relaxed and sleepy, put him back into his cot. Avoid any confusing or unsettling messages, so stay in your baby's room until he is asleep.

# Colds and viruses

Healthy babies have about six colds in their first year. Breastfed babies have fewer colds than formula fed babies, as breast milk contains antibodies and boosts baby's immune system, giving them extra protection from colds and viruses. However, when babies start to socialise with other babies at mum and baby groups or start at day nursery, catching a cold is unavoidable. Toddlers appear to have a constant cold for most of the year and their new baby brother or sister is vulnerable to catching their cold; therefore, breastfeeding new additions protects them from catching a cold from their sibling.

Babies are nose breathers and unable to breathe through their mouths until they are much older so a cold can affect their feeding and consequently sleeping pattern. To ease the problem, treat your baby's symptoms with decongestants suitable for babies and ensure your baby has positive sleep associations.

# Chapter fifteen

# *Weaning*

*"The philosophy behind baby-led weaning is that your baby instinctively knows which nutrients their body needs."*

Weaning is an important milestone in your baby's development, but not all mums enjoy the process or find it easy. My baby clinic was full of anxious mums worried about this subject. If weaning is rushed or forced, it can lead to food refusal and behavioural problems associated with food and eating. Weaning your baby onto solid food should be a fun process but it requires more thought and planning than just giving milk feeds.

### In this chapter:

- Baby-led weaning
- When to start weaning
- Recommended weaning foods
- Meal planner for babies aged six to nine months
- Meal planner for babies aged nine months to one year
- Meal planner for babies aged 12-18 months
- Common feeding problems

# Baby-led weaning

### What is baby-led weaning?

Baby-led weaning is a way of introducing solid food that allows babies to feed themselves. The philosophy behind baby-led weaning is that your baby instinctively knows which nutrients their body needs; offer food from each food group as your baby will choose the food their body requires. The advantage of baby-led weaning is that your baby learns to self-regulate their food intake, therefore is less likely to overeat and have weight problems in the future. Make every meal time enjoyable and a sociable event. Sit with your baby and eat together.

### When can I start?

From the age of four months, babies start to drool and watch you eating but this is not a sign to start weaning. Babies this age are developmentally not able to eat from a spoon and will push the food back out with their tongue. Before you introduce baby-led weaning, look for the signs that indicate that your baby is ready to self-feed. Your baby does not need to have teeth or be able to hold a spoon, as most babies will finger feed.

### What are the signs?

### Your baby should:

- Be able to sit up unsupported
- Have good eye and hand co-ordination
- Reach out to grasp for food, hold it in his fist and take it to his mouth
- Be able to chew and swallow

### What equipment will I need?

- A simple, adjustable high chair that is easy to wipe clean, has a removable tray and is easy to lift your baby in and out of

- A washable, protective floor mat placed under the highchair
- Small plastic feeding bowls, plates, spoons
- Sippy cups

### Self-feeding/finger-feeding

Babies from six- to nine-months-old are just having tastes, playing with their food and eating very little. The pincer movement of the index finger and thumb is developed by nine months, which makes finger-feeding much easier as babies can pick up peas and other small objects. Your baby will be a year old before being able to self-feed efficiently, therefore, milk, via breast/bottle, is their main food source. Learning how to use a spoon without the food falling off takes a lot of practice and, developmentally, babies are 15-18 months old before they can eat efficiently from a spoon.

### How long should my baby eat for?

Self-feeding is very tiring and babies rarely have enough interest to eat for longer than 20 minutes. Therefore, introduce your baby to nutritious, healthy foods from all the main food groups. See below.

Avoid giving water before the meal as this can depress your baby's appetite. Instead offer a drink the end of the meal from either a beaker or an open cup. After 20 minutes, mealtime is over; remove the food and take your baby down from the high chair. Finish their meal with a milk feed, breast or bottle. Be reassured, babies will only eat when they are hungry and drink when they are thirsty.

### Gag reflex

Babies naturally have a good gag reflex, but never leave your baby to eat on their own. I recommend all mums attend first aid classes to learn about what to do if their baby chokes. Look for a first aid class near you: redcrossfirstaidtraining.co.uk, sja.org.uk, milliestrust.com

From my own research into baby-led weaning, the evidence reports that most mums prefer a balance between offering their baby finger foods such as cooked and cubed meat, vegetables, fruit, pasta shapes, peas, rice cakes and giving their baby food from a spoon.

# Recommended first weaning foods

**Protein:**

| | |
|---|---|
| Meat: | beef, chicken, lamb, pork |
| Fish: | white fish, salmon (not shellfish) |
| Vegetarian: | well-cooked eggs, peas, beans, pulses, lentils, avocado, sweet corn |
| Milk: | cheese, yogurt, whole milk |

**Carbohydrate:** oats, rice, cereals, bread, potato, sweet potato, pasta

**Vegetables:** green vegetables, carrots, swedes, salad vegetables, cucumber, tomatoes, sweet peppers

**Fruit:** apples, pears, apricots, bananas, plums, peaches (strain fruits that have seeds)

### Foods to avoid

There are only a few foods to avoid until your baby is one year old, as they contain salmonella and other dangerous bacteria:

Any unpasteurised milk or cheese (French soft cheese), undercooked or raw egg, honey, raw shellfish, fish containing mercury and nuts in any form. Avoid giving processed foods that contain high levels of sugar, salt and saturated fat.

# Meal planner for babies aged six to nine months

If you are combining baby-led weaning with spoon feeding your baby, the consistency of food should be a thick purée, progressing to small, evenly sized lumps. Make every meal time a social event, sit and eat with your baby. NEVER leave your baby to eat alone.

Babies are recommended to have 600mls or 20 oz. of milk protein a day: add milk to cereal, sauces, and custards, (cheese and yogurts are made from milk) a small pot of yogurt contains 4 oz. (or 120ml) of milk; 30g (1oz.) of cheese is made with 8 oz. or 240 ml of milk.

### 6 to 7am

If your baby wakes, offer small milk feed breast/bottle.

### 8am Breakfast

Oat cereal, puréed fruit, fingers of toast spread with a thin layer of butter/margarine and jam or cream cheese. End the meal with a milk feed, breast or bottle.

### 10am

Water from a sippy beaker and Biscotti or similar.

### Midday Lunch

Fish/meat, milk protein, vegetables, and carbohydrate, fruit. End the meal with a milk feed breast or bottle. (Do not offer a drink before a meal as it will fill your baby's stomach with liquid and reduces the appetite.)

### 2pm

Water from a sippy beaker and small pieces of chopped fruit.

### 4pm Teatime

Pasta, milk protein, fruit and vegetables. End the meal with a milk feed breast or bottle.

### 7pm Supper

Carbohydrate, cereal and mashed banana or milk protein followed by a drink of water from a beaker. Avoid giving milk to drink at bedtime as it can become a milk-sleep association.

# Meal planner for babies aged nine months to one year

The consistency of the food should be small, evenly-sized lumps.

**6 to 7am**

Offer a small milk feed, breast or bottle, if your baby wakes up at this time and is too hungry to wait until breakfast.

**8am Breakfast**

Cereal, milk protein, fruit, toast. Drink of water in a beaker. Offer a milk feed, breast/bottle.

**Midday lunch**

Meat/fish protein, carbohydrate, milk protein (yogurt/cheese), vegetables, fruit. Drink of water.

**4pm Teatime**

Carbohydrate, yogurt/cheese, fruit and vegetables. End the meal with a milk feed, breast or bottle.

**7pm Supper**

Carbohydrate, yogurt, banana. Avoid giving milk to drink at bedtime as it can become a milk-sleep association.

Snacks are optional. Some babies do not want to eat between meals, but if your baby enjoys snacking, limit the amount and only offer water, a slice of fruit, one rice cake or similar.

# Meal planner for babies aged 12-18 months

From 12 months old, babies are very efficient at drinking out of a beaker, therefore, they do not need to drink from a bottle. Your breastfed baby may still want a breastfeed. As a general rule, babies eat the same cooked food as the family and the parent who cooks that day will often adapt a recipe to suit the baby. I recommend Annabel Karmel's *Baby and Toddler Meal Planner*, a very popular cookbook.

If your baby is at nursery, mealtime will be different. Nurseries usually give the children lunch between 11.30am and midday, and then a sandwich and fruit at 3.30pm. Adapt mealtimes to fit in with when you are eating.

**6 to 7am**
Small milk feed from a beaker.

**8am**
Cereal, fruit, yogurt, toast. Drink of water.

**10am**
Water from a beaker and snack.

**Midday**
Meat or cheese sandwich, salad vegetables, yogurt, fruit. Drink of water.

**2pm**
Water from beaker and snack.

**3.30pm**
Snack, yogurt or fruit.

**5 to 6pm**
Babies like to eat at the same time as the rest of the family and some mums will keep the milky dessert and give it to their baby later, before the bath.

# Common feeding problems

### Q. My six-month-old has started weaning, but has been waking up at 2am for a milk feed. Is he hungry?

**A.** Babies that have just started to wean often wake up in the night, hungry for a milk feed. The first thing to do is check your baby is having enough milk during the day: milk is more nutritious than fruit and vegetables, so aim to give your baby a milk feed before their solid food. Babies who are fussy with food and have small appetites should be offered fruit and vegetables foods with a higher calorie content such as banana, puréed sweet corn, avocado, sweet potato, squash, puréed peas, beans and lentils. If you want to increase calories without increasing volume, add a teaspoon of butter to the food.

When your baby is having three meals a day with meat or dairy protein, offer milk after the food. Your baby will feel fuller and will naturally reduce the amount of milk they need.

### Q. How much food should my baby eat at mealtime?

**A.** Babies' appetites vary considerably and some babies have bigger appetites than others; consequently, their stomachs have the capacity to hold more food. As a guide, if your baby drank 6-7 oz. (or 180-210ml) of milk at every feed time, that is the total volume of food or liquid to offer your baby. If your baby had a small appetite and only took 4 oz. (120ml) of milk at every feed time, that is the total volume of food or liquid your baby's stomach can retain. Any more and your baby could be sick.

If you were breastfeeding you wouldn't know the exact amount of milk your baby took, but you can use the above measurements as a guide. Baby-led weaning takes the decision and calculation away from parents allowing babies to regulate their own food intake at any mealtime.

**Q. My nine-month-old has three meals a day and milk feeds. How much milk should he have a day?**

**A.** Babies are recommended to have the calories and nutritional intake of 500mls of milk a day. This milk can be given as a drink, added to food or eaten. One small pot of fromage frais is made with 120mls of milk. 30g of cheese is made with 240mls of milk. Add milk to cereal and your baby will have the recommended amount.

**Q. My 14-month-old little boy, James, refuses to eat any cooked meals. He pushes the plate away and turns his face away. He will happily eat toast, yogurts, apple and pear purée and two pints of milk from a bottle. What do you suggest?**

**A.** When I met James, he looked a very healthy little boy as he was getting all the nutrition he needed from drinking two pints of milk a day. This was the first thing to change as he was filling up on milk and did not have the appetite to eat any other food. The approach we took with James was to stop pressurising him to eat. Previously, James had lots of attention at meal times, but he ate alone at a big kitchen table. His parents and grandparents cajoled and tempted him with the spoon all through the meal. They opened kitchen cupboards and made more meals in the hope he would eat them, which he did not. None of their interventions worked, so eventually they made him some toast which he ate beautifully. James had become very determined not to eat any hot meals made with red meat or tomatoes. James was able to regulate his appetite when he stopped drinking milk from a bottle. He was given his daily quota of milk in his breakfast cereal, grated cheese on his toast and in his yogurt. His family started to eat with him and left him with an empty plate with a communal plate for him to help himself; this approach allows children to make a choice about what and how much they want to eat. Young children are more likely to taste new foods if they see the family eating and enjoying the food. Babies and toddlers will eat when they are hungry and drink when they are thirsty and self-regulate how much they want to eat. It is the role of parents to offer nutritious, healthy food from all the main food groups.

# Chapter sixteen

# Frequently asked questions

Here are some questions I was frequently asked at my baby clinic.

## Feeding

**Q. How much food should my baby eat at mealtimes?**

**A.** Babies' appetites vary considerably and some babies have bigger appetites than others; consequently, their stomachs have the capacity to hold more food. As a guide, if your baby drank 6-7 oz. (or 180-210ml) of milk at every feed time, that is the total volume of food or liquid to offer your baby. If your baby had a small appetite and only took 4 oz. (120ml) of milk at every feed time, that is the total volume of food or liquid your baby's stomach can retain. Any more and your baby could be sick.

If you were breastfeeding you would not know the exact amount of milk your baby took, but you can use the above measurements as a guide. Baby-led weaning takes the decision and calculation away from parents and allows babies to regulate their own food intake at any mealtime.

**Q. My six-month-old has started weaning, but has been waking up at 2am for a milk feed. Is he hungry?**

**A.** Babies who have just started to wean often wake up in the night, hungry for a milk feed. The first thing to do is check your baby is having enough milk during the day. Milk is more nutritious than fruit and vegetables, so aim to give a milk feed before solid food. For babies who are fussy with food and have small appetites, I recommend they be offered foods with higher calorie content such as banana, puréed sweet corn, avocado, sweet potato, squash, puréed peas, beans and lentils. Without increasing the volume of food, add a teaspoon of butter to vegetables. When your baby is having three meals a day with meat or dairy protein, offer breast/ bottle after the food, and your baby will naturally reduce the amount of milk they need.

### Q. What is a dream feed?

**A.** A dream feed is the name for a late evening milk feed, given to your baby when he/she is asleep. A dream feed is usually given at 11pm. The reason for this is that it helps babies to sleep until 6am without waking for a feed. Parents lift their baby from the cot, give the feed while baby is asleep, gently wind and put baby back into the cot. The key to the dream feed is that baby is not aware of being fed so it does not become a habit and baby will gradually take less and less milk during the dream feed. It is not baby-led feeding, therefore not something I recommend when implementing a Multi-Sensory Sleep Routine.

### Q. At what age should my baby sleep through the night without needing a milk feed?

**A.** Most healthy, full term, two-month-old, breast or bottle fed babies have the potential to sleep from 11pm until 4-6am, or five to seven hours, without waking for milk. However, this average applies only to babies who can self-settle and have made positive sleep attachments.

### Q. My nine-month-old has three meals a day and milk feeds. How much milk should he have a day?

**A.** Babies are recommended to have the calories and nutritional intake of 500mls of milk a day. This milk can be given as a drink, added to food or eaten. One small pot of fromage frais is made with 120mls of milk. 30g of cheese is made with 240mls of milk. Add milk to cereal and your baby will have the recommended amount.

8am Breakfast: breast/bottle feed, plus cereal and fruit

Midday Lunch: balanced meal with meat protein, dairy protein, vegetables, fruit, and carbohydrate. Drink of water from a beaker

4pm Tea: Start with breast/bottle feed. Then offer meal with milk/protein, fruit, vegetables and carbohydrate

7pm Supper: Cereal and mashed banana (optional)

**Q. My 14-month-old little boy, James, refuses to eat any cooked meals. He pushes the plate away and turns his face away. He will happily eat toast, yogurts, apple and pear purée and two pints of milk from a bottle. What do you suggest?**

**A.** When I met James, he looked a very healthy little boy as he was getting all the nutrition he needed from drinking two pints of milk a day. This was the first thing to change as he was filling up on milk and did not have the appetite to eat any other food. The approach we took with James was to stop pressurising him to eat. Previously, James had lots of attention at meal times, but he ate alone at a big kitchen table. His parents and grandparents cajoled and tempted him with the spoon all through the meal. They opened kitchen cupboards and made more meals in the hope he would eat them, which he did not. None of their interventions worked, so eventually they made him some toast which he ate beautifully. James had become very determined not to eat any hot meals made with red meat or tomatoes. James was able to regulate his appetite when he stopped drinking milk from a bottle. He was given his daily quota of milk in his breakfast cereal, grated cheese on his toast and in his yogurt. His family started to eat with him and left him with an empty plate with a communal plate for him to help himself; this approach allows children to make a choice about what and how much they want to eat. Young children are more likely to taste new foods if they see the family eating and enjoying the food. Babies and toddlers will eat when they are hungry, drink when they are thirsty and self-regulate how much they want to eat. It is the role of parents to offer nutritious, healthy food from all the main food groups.

# Breastfeeding

**Q. My baby is three weeks old, but I want to be flexible and give my baby some of my expressed milk in a bottle. When is the best time to introduce this technique?**

**A.** If you are a new mum, don't start expressing until your baby is four weeks old, to ensure that breastfeeding is established and you are feeling confident about it. The best time to express your milk is after the first feed in the morning, between 6am and 8am. Use a manual, battery operated or electric breast pump, save the milk in the fridge and either use it within two to three days, or freeze it on the same day that it was expressed. Breastfed babies like a soft teat, so choose a brand that specialises in a breast/bottle style. The best time to give a breastfed baby a bottle of warmed expressed milk is in the evening, anytime from 8-11pm. This is a good time for dads to be involved in the feeding. Breastfeed during the night after you have had some sleep, as the prolactin levels are highest after deep sleep, milk production is good and your baby will have a good feed.

**Q. My three-month-old baby will only go to sleep if I breastfeed her. How can I stop this?**

**A.** Three-month-old babies who only fall asleep during a feed have developed a milk-sleep association. This is very habit forming, and as babies get older they become more dependent on breast milk to settle to sleep. The easiest way to stop this happening is teach your baby to self-settle without breastfeeding by following my Multi-Sensory Sleep Techniques for breastfed babies. Settle your baby to sleep without feeding, routinely give a breastfeed when your baby wakes up from a nap and give the last feed in the lounge, before the bath, as this prevents a milk-sleep association. If you are able to achieve this, hunger will naturally wake your baby.

**Q. My seven-month-old baby is fully breastfed and has started to take some solid food. I am going back to work in a month and want to stop breastfeeding and introduce formula in a bottle before I start work. When shall I make the switch?**

**A.** Most mums can continue to give one or two breastfeeds when they return to work, but if you want to stop breastfeeding, do it gradually to prevent engorgement and mastitis. Start to reduce the number of breastfeeds you give your baby two or three weeks before you return to work. The first breastfeed to stop is the lunchtime feed. Offer solid food and milk from a bottle or beaker. Allow your breasts to adjust to the change and, after a few days, stop another breastfeed at 7.30-8 pm. Offer milk in a bottle. If you feel your breasts are uncomfortable and engorged, express some milk until they feel comfortable. After a week, you will still be breastfeeding at approximately 6am, 10am and 4pm. The next feed to stop is the 10am breastfeed, then, three or four days later, the 4pm. Stop the last feed when you are ready.

**Q. My baby is four months old, fully breastfed and refuses to take a bottle or a dummy. How can I get her to take a bottle?**

**A.** The best way to encourage a four-month-old to take a bottle is to offer warmed, expressed milk in a bottle designed for breastfed babies. Wait until baby is hungry for a feed and get someone else to feed her, to prevent her from getting confused as to why you are not breastfeeding. She has to learn to suck in a new way as sucking a teat is very different to sucking your nipple. If you offer the bottle at bedtime every day, she will quickly learn how to suck the teat. Never force or pressurise her to suck the teat. That is counterproductive and will produce a negative association to the teat and bottle. With gentle perseverance, she will accept the bottle and take a small feed from it.

**Q. I think my baby is using my breast as a dummy. He is seven months old, on the 75 percentile for weight. I feed him three to four times in the night and five times during the day. I am exhausted. How can I stop this?**

**A.** Your baby is feeding like a newborn, and at seven months old, he is more than capable of sleeping for six hours without being fed. Breastfed babies are more likely to use the breast for comfort and sleep than bottle fed babies. Even breastfeeding mums can misinterpret communication with their baby. Popping babies on the breast for every whiny cry is not an appropriate response because babies can become completely dependent on the nipple for comfort and sleep.

1 Separate comfort breast feeds from milk feeds.

2 Aim to feed three-hourly during the day and as soon your baby uses the breast as a dummy, detach your baby – the feed is over.

3 When your baby is rubbing his eyes and yawning, instead of feeding, take your baby out for a short nap in the car or pram and when your baby wakes up, offer a breastfeed.

4 Introduce a comforter impregnated with your scent.

5 Aim to settle your baby in the nursery for at least one day nap without feeding.

6 Give your baby the last breastfeed before the bath, not after.

7 If your baby wakes before six hours, resettle him without a feed. Be flexible, as your baby might have a growth spurt (not every night, though).

8 Offer a milk feed if your baby wakes up after six hours.

# Sleep

### Q. At what age can my baby go into a cot?

**A.** Babies can go into a cot from birth. However, initially, most parents prefer to use a Moses basket or a crib for a few months. The ideal age to use a cot is three months. By then, most babies are too big for the Moses basket, touch the sides of the basket and wake themselves up. This is also an opportunity to use a battery operated mobile attached to the cot, as it encourages eye coordination and will entertain your baby until he/she is ready to go to sleep.

### Q What does the 'tired baby cry' sound and look like?

**A.** Your baby will look like this in the cot: his eyes are closed, no tears. He rolls about the cot trying to get comfortable, reaches for the comforter and rubs his face with it.

The cry can sound like this: it can start quiet and low, then get louder, as babies can get quite frustrated and resist going to sleep without their usual sleep associations i.e. rocking, patting or feeding. To prevent frustration developing, play, interact and distract your baby from getting upset. Use the distraction techniques until your baby starts the 'tired baby cry'. The tired baby cry is a grunting mantra-type cry. It is a stop-start cry – short bursts of crying, stopping for a few seconds, followed by another burst of crying. With each new cry, the volume decreases, the pauses get longer and within minutes your baby is asleep. It is very important that parents wait until their baby is tired enough to do this. Any anger or frustration in the cry shows your baby is not tired enough. If babies cry at every sleep time, they have not learnt how to self-settle and have a negative association with the cot and the nursery.

## Q What is a distraction technique?

**A.** All babies sound frustrated and unhappy when they learn new sleep associations. Being awake in the cot is a new experience for some babies. I recommend parents empathise and understand how difficult this is for their baby. Therefore, to make the process as easy for your baby as possible, apply distraction techniques. This requires patience, persistence and gentle perseverance.

Your baby's personality will determine how quick and easy it can be. Some babies have determined characters and resist being distracted. Some parents only needed to tap the side of the cot, click their fingers, move the Slumber Buddy light about the nursery or gently shake a rattle to get their baby's attention. Once you have stopped the cry, stop the distraction immediately. Reassure your baby with positive praise, and use the baby sign for OK and sleep (place your hands together and at the side of your face). Babies as young as five months recognise this sign and will understand what you want them to do.

Some older babies are not interested in looking at magic shows and need more distraction. Place a VTech toy like 'Alfie Bear', or similar, in the cot and switch it on for a second or two. VTech books that play nursery rhymes or animal noises are also very effective at distracting an older baby. Leave the book in the cot and let your baby play and press the buttons. Choose your baby's favourite toys. Your baby may want to play in the cot for 5-10 minutes before he is tired enough to sleep.

Once babies are truly tired and ready to self-settle, they will start the tired baby cry. Do not distract or intervene. Give them the time and the opportunity to self-settle. Once your baby has learnt how to self-settle, they will need to practise it five or six more times before it becomes a habit. Then your baby will settle down to sleep without a peep.

**Q. My baby goes in his cot awake and settles to sleep very well but wakes a few hours later. What can I do about this?**

**A.** This is a frequently asked question and the answer is if the bedtime routine was working your baby would not wake up during the night. When I have assessed the bedtime routine, I have noted that the parents are part of their baby's settling progress and their baby is not able to self soothe naturally. The parents are either giving the last feed after the bath, in the bedroom or nursery, or they are staying in the bedroom and interacting with their baby in some way. In every case I have dealt with, when the parents follow my bedtime routine and settling sequence and introduce the sensory sleep associations, every baby learns how to self soothe naturally and consequently sleep all night.

**Q. My 10-month-old son wakes up for the dummy three to four times a night. How can I stop this?**

**A.** Babies who wake up at night for their dummy have a dummy-sleep association. Dummies are very addictive and babies become very attached to them. To encourage him to put the dummy in himself, stop putting it in his mouth. To lessen the attachment, only use the dummy at sleep times and remove it from his mouth five minutes after sleep. When he wakes up crying for the dummy, go in and put it in his hand, encouraging him to put it in himself. If he throws it away, take the dummy away and leave the room, and wait outside the door. Let him protest for a minute, then go back in and put it in the cot, near enough for him to reach it. When he cries and indicates he wants you to get it for him, pat the mattress and say, "*Sleepy time, here's your dummy.*" Repeat the process until he has gone to sleep. This technique works very well and stops baby losing the dummy for attention. After a week, stop using the dummy for day sleeps and when this has been achieved stop using it at bedtime.

**Q. My son is 18 months old; he looks so tired, but refuses to have a day nap and just cries if I put him in his cot. It he overtired?**

**A.** He sounds an independent little boy and knows his own mind. Forcing him to have a nap is not going to work. He will continue to be very cross and angry and it could be counterproductive at that time. He would benefit from some relaxation and sensory playtime in the nursery.

After lunch, take him up to the nursery, but do not close the curtains. Switch on some relaxing, hypnotic music. Sit and read a story and have cuddles on your knee. Let him relax for at least 20 minutes. His world is very stimulating right now and he needs some quiet time away from constant activity. Sitting quietly with mummy is all some babies need. You never know, he might be so relaxed that he'll have a nap in the cot. If not, just go back downstairs. You have lost nothing but gained much more – you have both had a very nice time together.

**Q. What is an overtired baby?**

**A.** I know most mums are worried about their 'overtired baby' and some sleep experts recommend forcing babies to have day naps. In my experience, this practice is counterproductive and produces a negative sleep association. Most babies need a day nap to recharge their batteries. However, my approach to sleep is baby-led and this respects the natural individual sleep requirements of every baby. I encourage mums to wait until their baby is tired and not force or coerce the baby to sleep with a rock, pat or a feed. The best time for a day nap is half way through your baby's day. Some babies prefer a power nap in the morning, of about 20 minutes, then a longer nap lasting an hour just after lunch and another power nap before tea. I do agree that babies appear tired every two hours, but they can easily trick parents into thinking they are tired when, in fact, they are just bored and need a change of scene. Every baby benefits from a period of quiet sensory playtime every day. Consider what it is like for babies, learning new things everyday but having no control over their environment. There are so many developmental leaps in the first year. Babies are learning how to move, talk and make things happen at a tremendously fast rate and it is sometimes too much for their little bodies.

Overstimulation tires babies and this is why they need to relax and unwind with mummy in the nursery for at least 20 minutes' sensory playtime every day. This period of relaxation may not result in sleep, but it is a special bonding experience with your baby.

**Q. My baby is 11 weeks old, is still sleeping in the Moses basket and has started to wake up in the night. Is she hungry?**

**A.** Eleven-week-old babies who wake up in the night have outgrown the Moses basket. Babies grow very quickly and when your daughter can touch the sides of the Moses basket, the action disturbs her sleep. Once awake, she wants milk to go back to sleep. Start to use a cot now and you will see how comfortable she looks, and you will notice a huge difference in her sleep.

**Q. My baby is three months old and too big for the Moses basket, but I do not have space in my bedroom for a cot. I have read babies should sleep with their mums for six months. What shall I do?**

**A.** The average sized Moses basket is too small for babies over 12 lbs. So the dilemma is: where is the safest place for baby to sleep? Cot beds are too big for the average bedroom, so decide where you want your baby to sleep. A small cot or crib would fit most parents' bedrooms. If that is not an option for you, then a cot in the nursery is the safest place for baby to sleep. Place baby at the foot of the cot in a sleeping bag. Set up the baby listening monitor to give you reassurance.

**Q. My 16-month-old son wakes up screaming in the night, demanding a bottle of milk and in the process, wakes his sisters, aged 7 and 10 years. Can you help me?**

**A.** It is lovely to devote all your love, time and attention to your first child, but when you have more than one child to consider, bedtime can become tricky. Your time is divided. Where do you start? Jane could cope with her own personal lack of sleep, but the effect Joe had on her other children was something she would not tolerate and she wanted the best for all her children.

There was an added complication to this scenario: her little boy was extremely active and had climbed out of his cot when he was 14 months old. To prevent Joe injuring himself, he was sleeping in a junior bed, but kept getting out in the middle of the night and after a great deal of fuss and persistent crying, he ended up in mum's bed, while dad was relegated to the spare room.

The sisters adored their little brother and were like two little mothers to him, carrying him around and pandering to his every whim. They wanted him to sleep in their bedroom. The girls moved some furniture around in the bedroom to make room for his bed. It was very clear to me that the girls adored their little brother and treated him like a little prince. The girls created space for his bed and at bedtime Jane settled him using lights and nature sounds. Joe's sleep association was stroking Jane's hair until he was asleep. To discourage this Jane sat close by and gave him a teddy to stroke instead. Every time Joe tried to get out of bed, Jane encouraged Joe back in bed with firm but gentle persuasion until he eventually he fell asleep. He woke in the night, as this had been his habit for several months, but with more gentle perseverance and persistence and lots of "*Good boy... back into bed,*" he learned to stay in his bed all night. Sharing a bedroom worked for this family as everyone was in agreement about the arrangements. However, this may not work for every family.

### Q. How long will it take to teach my baby to self-settle and become an independent sleeper?

**A.** Babies learn to self-settle from the first sleep, but they require five to seven days practice before they sleep to their unique sleep potential. If the timing of sleep is right and the Multi-Sensory Routine is followed, then expect to see good results in two or three days.

### Q. My two-year-old has just started to sleep in a single bed, but she keeps crying and getting out of bed when I leave the room.

**I am up and downstairs for several hours until we are both exhausted and she eventually falls asleep. How can I stop this?**

**A.** Your toddler has separation anxiety. Encourage her to stay in her own bed by making the bedroom feel special and a nice place to be; have play times in there during the day, make the room multi-sensory and the best room in the house. Follow my Multi-Sensory Sleep Routine for toddlers.

Encourage your toddler to stay in bed with positive praise and immediate reward. Most two-year-olds can be irrational and unreasonable, therefore actions speak louder than words. You need bargaining tools like a sleep teddy or comforter, and stories. Some children respond very positively to a sleep toy such as a Slumber Buddy. The bedtime rule is that stories and sleep teddy stay in the bedroom and are only given when your toddler gets into bed. Say something like, "*As soon as you get into bed you can have teddy and a story.*" Reward your toddler for getting into bed, with immediate praise and giving the comforter or favourite teddy or reading a story. After the story, give one last kiss and cuddle, keep the night light on and leave the room. Wait outside the door, listening for movement. As soon as you hear your toddler getting out of bed, calmly walk back in, pick up teddy/comforter and say, "*As soon as you get into bed you can have teddy.*" Always follow through with what you say. Your toddler might test this a couple more times, but repeat this until she has gone to sleep. Stay friendly and calm at all times, follow the settling routine and your little one will be asleep in no time! In the morning, praise your child with a cuddle and hug. A star chart also reinforces good behaviour. Avoid rewarding with sweet treats or promising to buy a toy. The reward needs to be immediate and appropriate.

### Q. What is a sleep signal?

**A.** Never assume that your baby understands what you are doing. Although babies appear to be very alert and observant, they do not understand the complexities of adult behaviour. Without realising it, parents are very inconsistent and change their way of interacting with their baby unknowingly. Babies are very susceptible to any subtle change in the routine and will be upset and confused. Babies as young as five months old understand the baby sign for

'OK' and 'sleep' (place your hands together and at the side of your face). If you use sleep signs at every sleep time, your baby will settle much more peacefully. As babies develop, so does their language and comprehension. Babies nine months to one year understand 'Sleepy time' and 'Lie down', especially when you pat the mattress. If you want to signal to your baby that you are leaving the room, decide on a gesture to use. Before you leave the room, stroke their head or blow a kiss and say, *"Night-night, see you in the morning."* The bedtime saying I used with my girls was quite long-winded, but if I missed a bit out, they noticed.

**Q. My three-year-old cries if I do not lie down with him at bedtime and stay until he is asleep. He wakes up in the night and I end up getting back into his bed and falling asleep. In the morning, he is still tired, and has tantrums during the day. I am exhausted too. What else can I do?**

**A.** Any three-year-old who still wants mum or dad to lie with them at bedtime has become over-dependent for attention at sleep time. Kim, his mum, was his comfort blanket. Jake did not need this type of attention at sleep time. He appeared a very bright and intelligent little boy and liked to rule the roost and get his own way. His 18-month-old brother slept all night in his cot, therefore Jake could adapt to sleeping well too. Children who suffer broken and short bursts of sleep are very tired and irritable the next day. Jake was more than capable of becoming an independent sleeper. He would have more energy to play and be less tired and whiny during the day. Kim and Jake would both feel fresher in the morning ready to start a busy day.

Most three-year-olds have a good vocabulary and understanding, so discuss the changes with him. Be positive and upbeat about this; introduce a reward that will encourage his co-operation.

Make his bedroom multi-sensory and the best room in the house. Jake's bedroom was barren and bare. Follow the Multi-Sensory Bedtime Routine.

Settle Jake into bed, and then give him his favourite teddy to hug, and sit nearby to read the story. If he is truly tired he will be asleep in five minutes, so leave the room. If he is not asleep, wait in the room until he is asleep. Avoid eye contact and being drawn into any conversation. He will do anything to get you to react to him. In three or four days, Jake will feel confident, secure and happy enough to let you leave the room before he is asleep. Give him lots of praise and reward him with a 'Good boy' sticker in the morning.

**Q. I am about to start the Multi-Sensory Sleep Routines. I am nervous about what to expect.**

**A.** Parents are naturally nervous the first night. First, create a sensory sleeping environment and spend a few days getting everything together. Lower the cot mattress if your baby is over six months old. If your baby comfort breastfeeds, reduce this before you begin.

### First night

If parents start the routine too early, their baby will cry and become hysterical. I recommend parents start the routine 30-45 minutes later than normal. If the timing is right, babies start the 'tired baby' cry as soon as they are in the cot after the bath. Parents have commented that their baby enjoyed the sensory playtime in the nursery; their baby did not miss the milk feed after the bath and settled more easily than they expected. The parents are relieved and empowered by the new technique.

### How to respond during the night

If your baby has been waking persistently at the same time every night, that pattern of behaviour will continue for a few nights. Resettle your baby the same way as at bedtime. Your baby will adapt quicker to the new routine with positive reinforcement. Hungry babies normally wake between midnight and 4am, so aim to offer milk breast/bottle during that period, not before. You will still be present in the room, reassuring and distracting your baby from the escalating cry, but, normally, your baby will be asleep in half the time and sleep longer before waking up. It is important to be consistent and not change your interventions. Keep up positive reinforcement and resettle in the same way as bedtime.

### Second night

Babies settle much quicker than the first night, but there is still resistance. Babies usually sleep longer before waking.

### Third night

This is when a miracle occurs and your baby settles off to sleep with the minimum of fuss. It is still early days and nights! Consistency and perseverance are the key to success. Your baby has not reached his full sleep potential, which will develop in the next few nights. Quality night sleep affects the day naps; babies do not want a morning nap and are ready for a day nap halfway through their day. Let your baby lead his sleep; he has more energy to stay awake for longer between naps. Avoid coercing your baby to have a nap when they are not ready; one yawn and an eye rub is not a true sign of tiredness.

### Fourth night

Your baby has learnt how to self-settle but you are still part of the settling process; now is the time to retreat. If you have been moving the lights, or touching your baby while they settle, stop doing this and stand back from the cot, sit away out of sight and only respond if your baby sounds distressed. From experience, I have learned that some parents lean over the cot and are too eager to move the lights to distract their baby from crying. Position the light where your baby can see it and sit on the floor with your back away from your baby. Stay in this position until your baby is asleep and repeat this, if needed, during the night. Keep up the momentum and next time, move further away from the cot until you can put your baby in the cot and leave the room. When your baby is asleep, switch off lights and music. This will make a huge improvement to your baby's sleep potential.

### Fifth night

Leave the room before your baby is asleep. Only return if the cries escalate – give the sleep and thumbs up signs, and leave.

### After seven days

After seven days, your baby will be settling off to sleep very well and with the minimum of fuss. However, if you are still part of their settling process and a presence in the nursery, now is the time to back away and allow your baby to self-settle without you being in the room.

**Q. Help! My baby's sleep has regressed! We have been following the Multi-Sensory Sleep Approach for a few weeks. Bedtimes are so peaceful and calm now, but my baby has started to wake up again at 11pm. Any ideas?**

**A.** Waking before midnight is very significant as it identifies that babies have not learnt how to self-settle to the best of their ability. When babies wake at 11pm, they are still in REM sleep and easily roused. Sleep regression is common, especially when babies have entered a new developmental phase, such as rolling or pulling themselves up to a standing position, or have health problems such as colds and teething. Sleep regression also occurs when parents have stopped short of their goal or only implemented some of the techniques.

My advice is to follow the sleep routine for your baby's age as the settling techniques change slightly to take into consideration babies' developmental stages. I always urge parents to 'up their game' and take their baby to the 'next level of self-settling'. This will enable their baby to reach his unique sleep potential. More often than not, all the parent has to do is leave the room before their baby or toddler is asleep.

### Q. How shall I make a gradual retreat?

**A.** Gradually retreat from the nursery before your baby is asleep.

As soon as your baby settles down into a sleeping position, leave the room and wait outside, listening for movement. If your baby's cry escalates, go straight back in. Stay friendly and give reassurance with the key words and leave again. Repeat this until your baby settles to sleep. Gradual retreat for toddlers is different. As soon as your toddler settles into a sleeping position, whisper, "*Mummy's going to get a tissue. Stay in bed, mummy's coming back.*" Walk out and, a few seconds later, walk straight back in and stay in the room until your toddler is asleep.

Next night, stay out of the room for a minute before returning to stay until your toddler's asleep. Repeat this every night, increasing the time until your toddler can sleep without your presence in the room. The time it takes for this to be successful depends on the temperament of your child and also how tired they are.

### Q. I have been following the 'pick up, put down' and 'shush, pat' methods, but my six-month-old is fighting sleep and becoming increasingly upset with it. Shall I continue?

**A.** 'Pick up, put down' and 'Shush, pat' might work quite well for very young babies, but it is a habit that's very difficult to break. As babies get heavier, it becomes impractical and both mum and baby get very frustrated with it.

Stop it straight away and follow the Multi-Sensory Sleep Technique.

**Q. Should I worry about leaving my new baby to sleep in my bedroom during the day?**

**A.** It is very natural to be worried when you first leave your newborn to sleep on his own. However, the lounge environment is too stimulating for most babies, and it is not a practical place to leave a baby to sleep, with or without inquisitive toddlers or pets around. Also, it is important that babies should make a positive sleep association with the room they sleep in at night. Play soothing sleep music in the bedroom to encourage a positive sleep-sound association. Scent a comforter with your scent and leave it with your baby while they sleep. To help ease your worry and anxiety about leaving your baby, use a baby monitor that has a camera, so that your baby can sleep in peace and you have peace of mind.

**Q. I am teaching my baby how to self-settle. How do I respond to him when he wakes up during the night?**

**A.** Babies over six months old rarely wake up during the night hungry for milk. If they do wake up, it is for attention and because they need help to resettle themselves back off to sleep. Therefore, I suggest you do not feed your six-month-old baby before 4am. Babies over nine months do not need a milk feed before 6am.

If your baby wakes up before the milk feed is due, you respond to your baby in the same way as at bedtime but with less intervention. Your plan of action is to go to your baby when the cry is quite loud and it is evident he is not going to resettle himself, but not at the first peep.

If he is standing up in the cot, do not attempt to lie him down. If he is wobbly and unsteady on his feet protect him by padding the cot sides with cot bumpers in case he falls. Avoid talking, giving eye contact, picking him up or shushing. If you reach out to touch him this action could upset him as he will anticipate he is going to be picked up and he will cry even louder. Do not worry if he is standing up; when he is ready he will lie down by himself. Once you have checked he has just woken up and is not in pain or suffering from a high temperature, sit on the floor looking at him through the bars, take his comforter out of the cot and hold it. You are going to use it to entice him to lie back down in the cot. Avoid eye contact, Switch on the red glow light of the Slumber Buddy and sea sounds.

Say his name firmly and *"Sleepy time, lie down. Mummy's here,"* and pat the mattress. If he cries in response, repeat it enough times until he understands what you are saying. He will understand what you want him to do but he will resist as he is not used to you responding in this way. Depending on your baby's personality, the first night can be quite a challenging standoff and could go on for an hour, especially if he is particularly stubborn. But if you keep your position, stay calm and speak in a friendly, firm voice, he will lie down and go back off to sleep. He is tired and meant to be asleep. As soon as he lies down, give him his teddy/comforter and tell him he is such a good boy!

It might take an hour the first time, but patience and perseverance pay off. If you stay calm, your baby will be less frustrated and confused so by the second and third nights, he will not be waking and will be sleeping through the night.

If you are worried about illness and teething causing your baby to wake I recommend you read Chapter 14: What to expect with babies with health problems.

## Day naps

### Q. How long should my baby nap for during the day?

**A.** Newborn babies nap most of the day, then as their circadian sleep rhythms change, they have longer periods of being awake during the day. Babies who have short, frequent day naps are not receiving the best sleep available to them. Putting your baby down for a nap every couple of hours will upset your baby, cause resistance and behavioural problems with sleep, as mums resort to feeding, rocking or patting their baby to sleep. From three months of age, most babies have three separate day naps, three to four hours apart, each one lasting perhaps 45 minutes to an hour.

From six months, babies can stay awake for longer and most only need two day naps, four to five hours apart. To ensure your baby has the best quality sleep, aim for each nap to be at least an hour long.

From 12 months, babies benefit from one day nap half way through their day, normally after lunch and lasting at least an hour.

Babies from one to two years still need day naps to keep their energy levels high, but they are energised by a shorter day nap. Avoid letting your 18- to 24-month-old have long day naps, as it will impact on the number of hours they sleep at night.

**Q. I like to go out during the day, so my six-month-old baby has catnaps in the car or pram. How can I make my baby sleep for longer?**

**A.** Catnaps are great for cats but not great for babies. Babies need at least one block of quality sleep a day, lasting an hour or more.

To help your baby to sleep for longer, introduce a comforter/sleep toy, which your baby can associate with sleep. Give the comforter/sleep toy to your baby at every naptime. If your baby is due a sleep before you are due to go out, settle your baby to sleep in the pram or car seat before you go, then, when you are ready, carry baby to the car. He might stir, but will quickly go back to sleep with the motion of the car. Doing that will ensure your baby can reach his unique sleep potential.

**Q. My 18-month-old baby and my three-year-old regularly have a 20 minute power nap in the car at 5pm on the way home from nursery and they both fight bedtime sleep at 7pm. What can I do about this?**

**A.** Falling asleep on the way home from nursery is often unavoidable. The children have had a power nap, therefore they will not ready for bed at 7pm. Children need to be awake for at least three to four hours before they are ready for baby-led sleep and the Multi-

Sensory Bedtime Routine. Bedtime could vary from night to night, depending on how much sleep the children have during the day. Bedtime could be 7.30pm one night and 8pm the next. Be flexible.

As soon as you are home, prepare your children for sleep time, gently wake up them up and let them settle into their change of environment. Let them play and use up lots of energy for at least an hour. Start the Multi-Sensory Sleep Routine when you see the tired signs.

**Q. I am worried about leaving my new baby to sleep in my bedroom during the day.**

**A.** It is very natural to be worried when you first leave your newborn to sleep. However, the lounge environment is too stimulating for babies and it is not a practical place to leave a baby to sleep with or without inquisitive toddlers or pets around.

In addition, it is important that babies should make a positive sleep association with the room they sleep in at night. Play soothing sleep music in the bedroom to encourage a positive sleep-sound association. Scent a comforter with your scent and leave it with your baby while he sleeps. To help ease your worry and anxiety about leaving your baby, use a baby monitor that has a camera so your baby can sleep in peace and you have peace of mind.

## Behaviour

**Q. When is the best time to start toilet training?**

**A.** By two years of age, most children indicate they have a dirty nappy by patting their nappy and saying, "*Poo.*" They understand when mum says, "*You've done a poo. Mummy change your nappy.*" At this stage, your child thinks it is normal to poo/wee in the nappy and mummy changes the nappy. Now is the time to have a new conversation with your child such as, "*Wees and poos can go in the potty.*" Make it a fact and not a request, as it might be too early for your child to be developmentally capable of using the potty successfully. If your child has not indicated they are ready, wait a few more weeks, but on average, the best time to start toilet training is at age two-and-a-half. Some children, although ready to use the potty, prefer to use the nappy to wee/poo. I once knew a three-year-old boy who preferred to play with his cars in the lounge while he dirtied his nappy. This was not really appropriate for his age and when his mum saw him starting to strain she took him to the bathroom where he finished having a poo and his nappy could be changed. Being proactive prepares your child for the next phase, sitting on the potty.

If your child is ready, most children are toilet trained within a week. Here is a plan of action:

- Have fun choosing new pants together and have several to hand in case of accidents

- Older children like rewards and a sticker chart is a great incentive during the first week; it is an immediate and visual reminder of their achievement

- Your child will have fewer accidents and be toilet trained quicker if you plan to be close to home for a few days as repetition and continuity speed up the process

- Stop using a nappy or pull-up during the day, even when you go out as pull-ups are counterproductive to toilet training; when your child is wearing a pull-up, the sensation on their skin is the same as a nappy

- If your child is not dry at night, they may need a nappy for a day nap; children wee in REM sleep

- Take your child to the potty after a drink or after meals. Say, "*Let's see if a wee wee comes?*" Only sit your child for a minute or longer if they are happy to do so. If nothing happens, say, "*Try again later.*"

- Little boys need to learn to wee and poo on the potty, otherwise they will continue using the nappy for a poo; when little boys are fully toilet trained, they can stand up to pass urine. It is very common for little boys to be dry during the day and night, but poo their pants or bedtime nappy

- By the end of the first week, your child will tell you when they need the potty and prefer you to wait outside the bathroom. They will shout "*Ready!*" when they want you to help with wiping and pulling up pants

By the age of two years and six months, the muscle that controls the release of urine has matured and children are able to recognise the urge to wee and they can hold on until they have reached the potty. Some children have accidents and get to the potty a little too late – be very sensitive to little accidents as children are very upset if they think they have done something wrong; say, "*Never mind, next time in the potty.*" Being critical or impatient can lead to behavioural issues with using the potty; conversely, avoid drawing too much attention and using over exaggerated praise when your child does a wee in the potty. A cuddle and pat, with, "*Well done, clever boy*" is enough praise. Avoid involving other family members in front of your child as too much attention is very intimidating and makes children self-conscious. Some children like all the praise and attention and try to use the potty again and fail; this confuses and disappoints children. Normalise going to the potty and let your child see you use the toilet and the actions involved – wiping, flushing the toilet and washing hands.

**Where to keep the potty:**

Children of two years are quite accepting of using the potty in the lounge even in front of other people, while older children become self-conscious and embarrassed, in which case, keep the potty in the bathroom.

Once your child is confident using the potty, keep up the momentum and progress to a toilet seat and step.

**Dry at night:**

During Non-REM sleep (midnight until 4am), a hormone is produced to condense urine, which aids dry nights. This hormone is not present in every child under school age. Enuresis is a hereditary condition. However, if you know of a close family member who had enuresis, be reassured; there is help available from specialist school nurses. Most children are dry at night before they are five years old.

You will know if your child has produced the hormone and condensed the urine. The nappy will feel light and dry in the morning. You can tell if your child has just had a wee in the nappy, as it will be very warm and very wet. If you think your child is ready to stop using nappies at bedtime, use a mattress protector in case of accidents. Discourage your child from drinking more than a few ounces of juice/water/milk at bedtime or during the night as it will compromise the chance of dry nights.

**Regression**

Sometimes the novelty of using the potty wears off, especially in little boys. Some are too busy playing and leave it to the last minute and have accidents. Others have a lazy streak in their nature and are not bothered about where or when they have a wee/poo. Often, they just need reminding about what is expected of them and more positive praise. A sticker or star chart will help to keep their focus and interest. Toilet regression also occurs when there has been any major change in their life, such as a new baby in the family, moving house, or starting play group or nursery, all of which are a normal part of life and, therefore, after a period of adjustment, the problem resolves itself.

**Q. My 13-month-old starts to gag and makes himself sick if I do not pick him up out of the cot and lie with him on my bed. This behaviour started when I left him to cry and since then, he's started to gag and vomit every time I put him in the cot. What can I do?**

**A.** Some babies deliberately gag and make themselves sick. This is extreme learned behaviour, stressful for you and your baby.

Your baby has learned that if he gags or makes himself sick, you will respond to his demands. The first time a baby vomits, parents are naturally upset, react, and respond to the behaviour. Any reaction from the parent reinforces the behaviour and baby learns that vomiting brings lots of attention.

The first thing to do is establish the Multi-Sensory Sleep Approach, set up a multi-sensory nursery and implement the Multi-Sensory Sleep Routine and sequencing.

The key to success is distraction. As soon as you see him gagging, use distractions to prevent him being sick. Try to be neutral, calm and friendly and not show any emotion. Any attention will reinforce the behaviour.

Encourage him to lie down in the cot and reward him when he lies down in the cot. The reward can be a comforter, a favourite toy anything that will capture his interest, distract and calm him. Remove the distraction when he stands up in the cot. Only let him see or feel the distraction when he is lying down. It should be something interesting and distracting, but also calming. Some mums use Smartphone apps for nursery rhymes on their mobile phones or laptops; only use them as a reward when baby is lying down.

Mobile apps are not to be used every day, and are only until your baby has adjusted to the new routine and learned to self-settle in the cot.

Keep up the distraction technique until your baby relaxes and settles to sleep. After three or four days, your baby should have stopped gagging to make himself sick and learnt how to self-settle.

### Q. My 14-month-old baby head bangs the cot when I leave him at sleep time. Is he hurting himself?

**A.** Head banging is learned attention-seeking behaviour. Some babies will do it if they are annoyed or frustrated and it is a form of self-distraction. Babies do not deliberately hurt themselves. When babies first do this, their parents are naturally upset, react, and respond to the behaviour. Any reaction from the parent reinforces the behaviour and baby learns that head banging gives him lots of attention.

If the head banging is associated with sleep time, begin by establishing a multi-sensory bedroom and Multi-Sensory Sleep Routine.

Don't rush to put baby down to sleep. Wait until he is ready to go down into the cot, and sit with him in the nursery for 20 minutes a day for play time sessions and have 10 minutes relaxing with stories before every sleep time. Your baby will stop head banging when he realises head banging is not getting him any attention.

### Q. We were in such a good routine and I could read my baby's signals, but she has changed and I do not know what she wants now. What has happened?

**A.** Your baby has made a developmental leap, and is making a transition from one phase of development to another. In my own personal experience and from observation, it occurs when babies are mentally and emotionally ready to do more than they are physically capable of, such as wanting to crawl or talk. This lead to days of frustration, until babies have mastered a new skill.

Parents can inadvertently delay their baby's progress to move onto the next phase of physical, psychological, social and emotional development. I have heard comments like, "*He's my last so I want to keep him a baby for longer.*" When your baby has developed a new capability towards independence e.g. self-feeding or self-settling, this should be encouraged, as this is the natural learning process for babies and children.

**Q. My six-month-old baby has not made an attachment to any toy or comforter, but he likes to hold my top when he feeds. Is he too old to have one now?**

**A.** Babies only make attachments to comforters if they are given the opportunity to do so. Babies are easier to settle if they have a comforter. Choose one your baby will like and keep it down your bra while you are feeding. Allow your baby to feel and stroke the comforter while they are feeding. It will absorb your natural scent. If you give it to your baby at every sleep time, within a few days, your baby will have made a sleep attachment to the comforter.

# Health

**Q. My one-year-old has been in hospital for a small operation and now she screams if we leave her at bedtime.**

**A.** Babies who have been sleeping well often regress when they have had an upsetting experience. If the operation is planned, take with you their sleep teddy/comforter. Stay with your baby until they have been anaesthetised and be in the room when they come out of recovery. When you are home, keep to your usual bedtime routine, but spend more time in the nursery before the bath. After the bath, settle your baby in the usual way. If your baby cries and clings to you, stay in the room until she goes to sleep. You might have to continue reassuring your baby for a few more nights until the upsetting memory fades. After three or four days, make a gradual retreat and leave the room before your baby is asleep.

### Q. My nine-month-old has eczema and the eczema seems to get worse after a bath. Shall I stop bathing at bedtime?

**A.** Dermatologists recommend that babies with dry skin and eczema should have a daily bath to remove flakes of skin and to prepare the skin for the emollients. Bath water can irritate and dry out baby's skin, so reduce the itch caused by the drying effect of water by adding bath emollient to the water and apply emollient cream to baby's skin before going in the bath. Extra care is needed, as baby will be slippery and take care as the bath will be slippery too.

After the bath, gently pat the skin dry and apply more emollient cream and if prescribed, treatment cream such as hydrocortisone. Use greasy creams and ointments at bedtime, as they are easily absorbed on warm, moist skin.

It may take 20 minutes for baby to feel comfortable after the bath, in which case, bath your baby at another time and do not make the bath part of the sleep routine.

### Q. My three-week-old baby has colic and reflux and he prefers to sleep on my chest. He cries if I put him down. What can I do about this?

**A.** Babies with colic and reflux are fussy, irritable babies and parents will do anything to settle their distressed baby. However, by six months of age, most babies have outgrown colic and reflux, but are still sleeping on mum or dad. They now have a sleeping problem caused by colic and reflux. The first thing to do is get the correct diagnosis and treatment, consult your GP for treatment and once you have started treatment, start to implement my Multi-Sensory Techniques. The Multi-Sensory Sleep Approach is perfect for colicky babies. Introduce a comforter so your baby can make an attachment to it. Soft glow and interesting lights will distract your baby from crying. Playing soothing sleep music will relax and calm your baby.

## Q. What is colic?

**A.** The medical term 'colic' describes the pain humans sometimes feel in the smooth muscle of either their bowel or kidney. However, in babies, the term colic commonly describes a type of cry and behaviour babies exhibit when they have trapped wind. Babies' bowels are extremely active; milk is constantly being digested and the waste product of milk produces lots of gas and wind. Most babies are not disturbed by this normal biological process, but some more sensitive babies feel the sensation more acutely and cry with discomfort. Babies with a feeding problem, constipation, allergy to cows' milk or milk intolerance produce more wind than is comfortable for them, and the pressure in the bowel causes increased discomfort and pain. To confirm diagnosis, they will cry after every feed and even whimper, jerk and grimace in their sleep. Their colic will not be resolved until the feeding problem has been treated. Obviously, not all babies have a feeding problem associated with colic pain; it is difficult to differentiate between colic pain caused by a feeding problem and colic caused by constipation or trapped wind. Many babies are given the term 'evening colic' to describe their crying in the evening. Every evening at around 6 pm, they start to have bouts of inconsolable crying. The pain of colic and the cry of an overtired, irritable baby can seem identical. When babies cry, they screw up their faces, look red in the face and move their arms and legs about in a very agitated way. Babies with 'evening colic' are often babies with sensitive personalities. Their colic can be relieved with a warm, deep bath and abdominal baby massage. My Multi-Sensory Sleep Techniques help to distract, settle and soothe babies with colic. Fortunately 'evening colic' resolves itself without treatment by three to four months of age.

## Q. When do babies start to teethe?

**A.** At birth, the first teeth are deep in the jaw bone and start to move up to the gum line from three months old. This is the age when parents notice their baby dribbling and rubbing their gums with their fist. Three-month-old babies have entered into a new phase of development. They have learned how to put their hands in their mouth and they produce more saliva in preparation for weaning. Babies continue to dribble and drool until two years of age or until their back molars have erupted. When babies are teething, they can look hot, flushed, and whiny and have one red cheek. Just to complicate matters, the baby might also have a cold, with a runny nose and watery eyes, as babies can experience six consecutive colds in the first year of life. A mixture of symptoms can confuse parents and they worry more. My recommendation is parents first treat the symptoms their baby presents with. If their baby feels hot, give a drink of cool water and, to reduce the fever and ease any pain, give the recommended dose of Paracetamol or similar pain-relief for babies. Within 20 minutes, the symptoms should have resolved and your baby will be happy and content again.

### Q. When will I see the first tooth?

**A.** Very rarely, babies are born with a tooth but, on average, most babies have their first tooth by their first birthday. The first teeth are tiny, they have serrated edges and are very sharp. Most mums only notice their baby has a tooth when they are bitten! The bottom two teeth pop through first, followed by the top two teeth. From three months of age until two years, babies are, in effect, teething for nearly two years. It is a normal phase of development and most babies cope well with teething. It does not disturb their sleep if they already have a good sleep routine and can self-settle. However, those babies that need parental intervention at sleep times may have increased waking during teething.

### Q. What should I do if teething wakes my baby in the night?

**A.** Firstly, implement the Multi-Sensory Sleep Routine appropriate for your baby. Secondly, when your baby wakes in the night with the symptoms described above, treat the symptoms. Then sit together in the nursery for 20 minutes, look at the red glow light and listen to soothing ocean sea sounds. When the pain and discomfort has passed and your baby is relaxed and sleepy, put him back into his cot. Avoid any confusing or unsettling messages, so stay in your baby's room until he is asleep.

Resources

# Recommendations

The following products are parent recommendations:

## Cot wedges and support for babies with reflux
* Baby Anti Rollover Sleep Positioner Infant Support Cot Safety Pillow
* Direct2Mum Moses Basket Cot Wedge (28cm)

## Teether
* Sophie the Giraffe Original Teether

## Baby comforter blankets
* Baby Sense Taglet Security Blanket
* Gro Comforter Percy Penguin/Lottie Lamb
* Elli & Raff Giraffe Soft Plush Baby Comfort Blanket

## Sensory sleep toys, lights and mobiles
* Summer Slumber Buddies: Bella Butterfly, Eddie Elephant and Frankie-Frog
* Seahorse by Fisher Price
* Ewan the Dream Sheep
* Rainforest Peek-a-Boo Leaves Musical Mobile by Fisher Price
* Innoo Tech LED Star Night Light Projector Lamp, Colourful Starry Night, Bed Side Lamp

## Books at bedtime
* Each Peach Pear Plum by Janet and Allan Ahlberg
* Five Speckled Frogs by Debbie Tarbett

**Interactive distraction cot toys for babies aged six months**

- LeapFrog My Puppy Pal
- VTech Baby Sing and Discover Piano
- Halilit Rainbow Spinner musical instrument
- VTech Baby Moosical Beads
- VTech Little Singing Alfie/Cora
- VTech Baby Crawl and Learn Bright Lights Ball

**Cot toys for sensory play time**

- Lamaze Play & Grow Freddie the Firefly
- Very Hungry Caterpillar developmental toys
- My 1st Baby Spiral Cot Activity Hanging Toy for cot
- Pop-Up Farm Friends

**For the bath**

- Tippitoes Mini Bath (newborns)
- Munchkin White Hot Inflatable Duck Tub
- BabyDam Bathwater Barrier

**Bath toys**

- Soft Bath Book Baby Toddler
- Child's Bathtime Play Floating Educational Toy
- TOMY Aquafun Octopals
- Munchkin Sea Squirts

**Toddler**

- Gro-Clock Sleep Trainer

**Bottles for breastfed babies**

- Tommee Tippee Closer to Nature Feeding Bottles

**Highchair**

- BabyBjorn Highchair

**Feeding cups, beakers and bowls**

- Bickiepegs Doidy Cup
- Tommee Tippee Explora Easy Drink Cup
- Munchkin Stay Put Suction Bowls
- Vital Baby Basics Simply Everything You Need Kit

# References

1  Burnham, M. M., Goodlin-Jones, B. L., Gaylor, E.E., and Anders, T.F. (2002). Nighttime sleep-wake patterns and self-soothing from birth to year one of age: a longitudinal intervention study. Journal of Child Psychology and Psychiatry, 43(6), 713-725

2  Galbally, M., Lewis, A. J., McEgan, K., Scalzo, and Islam, F.A. (2013). Breastfeeding and infant sleep patterns: an Australian population study. Journal of Paediatrics and Child Health, 49:E147-E151

3  Henderson, J.M., France, K. G., Blampied, N. M. (2011). The consolidation of infants' nocturnal sleep across the first year. Sleep Medicine Reviews. 15:211-220

4  Hiscock, H., (2010). Rock-a-bye-baby? Parenting and infant sleep. Sleep Medicine Review. 14:85-7

5  Hotelling, B. A., (2004), Styles of Parenting. The Journal of Perinatal Education. Winter, 13(1): 42-44

6  Koukis, M. (2009). Pregnancy Dreams. In: S. Krippner and D. Joffe Ellis. Perchance to Dream. New York: Novea Science Publishers, Inc.

7  Martin, J., Hiscock, H., Hardy, P., Davey B., Wake, M. (2007).Adverse associations of infant and child sleep problems and parent health: an Australian population study. Pediatrics, 119, pp. 947–955

8  McNamara, Patrick. International Journal of Childbirth Education. 27.1 (Jan 2012): 58-63

9  Meijer, A. N., (2010). Infant Sleep Consolidation: New perspectives. Sleep Medicine Reviews. Volume 14, Issue 2, Pages 85–87

10  Quinn (2004), From Pram to Primary. University Press

# Biography

Evelyn was born in Lanark, Scotland and her family moved to Cheshire when she was 11 years old. She met her husband Paul when she was 16 and they were married 3 years later in 1975.

She studied and worked as a nurse and midwife at Leighton Hospital, Crewe and trained in Manchester in 1981 as a health visitor.

11 years after her marriage her daughter Sophie was born and then exactly 2 years and 35 minutes later Emma was born. The family lived in Hartford Cheshire until Evelyn was widowed in 2009. She continued working as a health visitor in Middlewich Cheshire until her early retirement in 2011.

Since her retirement Evelyn has focused all her energies in helping parents with baby sleep problems and is known in the area as the Cheshire Baby Whisperer™. She supports families either by making home visits or gives advice and support over the telephone and answers questions via email.

**You can connect with Evelyn on social media or via her website:**

 twitter.com/CBWhisperer

 facebook.com/groups/cheshirebabywhisperer

 cheshirebabywhisperer.com

18671255R00157

Printed in Great Britain
by Amazon